REFUEL

Strengthen Your Soul, Energize Your Mission

BY ROB PARKMAN

Produced by:

FriesenPress

Suite 300 — 990 Fort Street

Victoria, BC, Canada V8V 3K2

www.friesenpress.com

Distributed to the trade by The Ingram Book Company

TABLE OF CONTENTS

Preface i

Introduction: Forgetting to Fuel Up iii

PART ONE: IS IT WELL WITH YOUR SOUL? xi

One: Running on Empty 1

Two: What Drains Your Tank? 9

Three: Who Pulled the Plug? 23

Four: The Hope of Replenishment 35

PART TWO: PLANNING FOR REPLENISI IMENT 49

Five: Renewing Your Mind 51

Six: Forgiving Your Debtors 63

Seven: Choosing Your Friends = Choosing Your Future 75

Eight: Permission to Rest 87

Nine: Nourishing Your Spiritual Life 97

Ten: Increasing Your Physical Capacity 109

Eleven: Creating a Life-Giving Marriage 119

Twelve: De-stressing Your Finances 131

Thirteen: Re-focusing On Your Calling 147

Conclusion: Becoming Resilient 169

Resource One: My Replenishment Strategy 175

Resource Two: Replenishment Verses 177

Resource Three: Recommended Reading 181

For Camille —
You refresh people wherever you go.
I am blessed to call you my own.

PREFACE

Ninety-five percent of people who pick up this book will agree that they need refuelling immediately, *and the other five percent are in denial!*

I am in your corner. I know what it is like to be desperate for renewal in my own personal and professional life. I want to help you identify the ways that your soul and your passions are being depleted. I want to show you the *real world solutions* I have found so that you can come up with your own replenishment strategy that will work where the rubber meets the road in your life.

More importantly, God is in your corner. He is for you. *Knowing that changes everything.* Read on and find out how He has generously provided everything that you need for your ongoing renewal.

At the end of each chapter you will find questions for discussion and reflection. I encourage you to discuss what you are learning with your spouse, a friend, your leadership team or your small group. Also, be sure to take advantage of the replenishment resources in the appendix.

It's time to refuel!

INTRODUCTION:
FORGETTING TO FUEL UP

"For I will satisfy the weary soul, and every languishing soul I will replenish." Jer. 31:25

It was an awkward situation. My wife, Camille, and I had left our boys at summer camp for a night while we made a run into the next province for a ministry booking at a church. On our way back to pick up the boys the next day we realized that we were getting low on fuel. Fortunately we were passing through a city on the way to camp, so we made the mental note to fuel up. We would need a full tank of gas to get us home later that night.

However, when we got to the city, we remembered that there was a great sale on DeWalt drills. I ran to do my manly errands while Camille picked up a few other items we needed. Then, since it had been a while since we had been in civilization, we had to scout out a good cup of coffee. Finally, we went off happily to camp with latte froth on our upper lips.

But we had forgotten to fuel up!

That night at camp we decided we would stay for the evening service. After that we talked and laughed with old friends for hours. It was after midnight when we finally pulled away from camp — Camille driving our van and myself driving our truck and pulling my Dad's boat.

After being on the highway for some time, I looked down and saw that the fuel gauge in the truck was nearing 'empty'. We didn't have enough fuel in the truck to get home. Right about then, Camille started flashing her lights at me, signalling me to pull over because she was also very low on fuel. There on the side of the road while watching the spectacular northern lights, we shook our heads and smiled at each other and our boys because of the situation we had gotten ourselves into. All of the gas stations in the area had closed hours earlier.

Just then, our youngest son blurted out, "Doesn't Grandpa's boat have fuel in it?!"

He was right! *We hadn't realized that what we needed was right there. The fuel was available, but we had to access it.*

I pulled the fuel tank out of the back of the boat and did the best I could to transfer fuel into the truck and the van. Thankfully, there were no environmental protection agents lurking in the ditches as I was working without a funnel. More importantly, though, we were thankful that we didn't have to spend the night on the side of the road!

HOW FULL IS YOUR TANK?

Imagine that you and I are sitting down for a coffee (no, neither of us have froth on our upper lips!). I'm sitting across from you and asking, "*If you were honest, how full would you say your emotional tank is right now? Have you been remembering to refuel?*" How would you answer?

How full is your tank?

You probably know what it is like to walk around sometimes with your tank on 'empty'. Having a depleted soul is a horrible thing. I know what it is like to be 'running on fumes'. Perhaps you have had your energy siphoned away by such influences as:

- physical exhaustion

- family dysfunction

- economic disadvantage

- health challenges

- organizational politics

- unhealthy personal habits

- thoughtless comments

- debilitating misbeliefs

- relational friction

Sadly, you often don't realize that you are depleted until the tank gets dangerously low. You find yourself feeling fatigued and burnt out. You can't get motivated. You lose interest in activities that used to bring you joy. You struggle to maintain a sense of hope and optimism. You lose your vision. You blame others. You express anger that is out of proportion to the circumstances. You withdraw and isolate yourself. You turn to activities you know you will regret later

Your 'low fuel' lights have been flashing for a while, but you push on. Few of us want to admit that we are feeling spiritually, mentally and/or physically depleted — but *you do need to refuel.*

If you are in denial — and most high achievers are — I want to awaken you to the dangers of not caring for your soul.

If you are not sure how you got to this point — I want to help you understand what drains you and what to do about it.

If you are feeling drained — and most leaders are — I want to show you how you can and will be replenished.

If you feel alone in the journey — and many of us do — I want to introduce you to flesh and blood characters in the Bible who felt what you feel.

If you are feeling like there is little hope of feeling better — I want to imprint on your mind the promises of God that you will be restored.

If you are not sure where to go from here — I want to help you design your own custom plan for renewal that is based on what 'fills your tank'.

REASONS FOR HOPE

Negative circumstances in life can leave you feeling deflated and defeated. In *"Part One: Is It Well With Your Soul?"*, we look in greater depth at the draining influences in your life. You have to identify the 'leaks' in your tank so that you can address them. It can be very difficult to have an honest look at what is draining you, but it is absolutely necessary. Do not get bogged down in Part One! In *"Part Two: Planning For Replenishment"* we look at the ways that God has provided for us to top up our tanks. You have many reasons for hope. If you access all that God has made available, in the end you will be able to say "my cup overflows" (Ps. 23:5).

I want to start on a note of hope and confidence so that you are ready roll up your sleeves and dive into Part One. One of the main keys to refuelling, as we will discover, is *increasing your ability to absorb and appropriate the life-giving promises of Scripture.* I want you to receive hope by finding a quiet space and meditating on Jeremiah 31:25, where God says:

> *"For I will satisfy the weary soul, and every languishing soul I will replenish."*

At the time this promise was given, God's people were going into a period of captivity. The prophet Jeremiah's heart was broken. His people were unaware of the misery that awaited them because of their unwillingness to return to God. But God wanted them to know that this wasn't the final chapter for his people. God reminded Jeremiah that there was a time of *restoration* coming for them. Jeremiah, and the people of God, needed to know that in the end *God would tend to the heart of each person that had become discouraged and depleted through what they had experienced.* God is, by nature, *for* them:

> *"Great is the LORD, who delights in the welfare of his servant!" (Ps. 35:27)*

In the meantime, *they were to meditate on and anticipate the fulfillment of each promise that was on its way towards them.* By these assurances and promises (found in Jeremiah 31:3-5 & 9-14), they would be nourished and sustained:

> *You have been the object of His care up to this point* — "I have loved you with an everlasting love."

> *You will continue to experience His undying commitment to you* — "Therefore I have continued my faithfulness to you."

You will be personally rebuilt by God — "Again I will build you, and you shall be built."

You will have your joy restored — "Again you shall adorn yourself with tambourines and shall go forth in the dance of the merrymakers."

You will prosper and be provided for — "The planters shall plant and shall enjoy the fruit... I will make them walk by brooks of water."

You will be secure and stable — "...in a straight path in which they shall not stumble".

You will be fathered and kept by God — "For I am a father to Israel... (I) will keep him as a shepherd keeps his flock."

You will be delivered by God — "For the Lord has ransomed Jacob and has redeemed him from hands too strong for him."

You will be revived — "and they shall be radiant over the goodness of the Lord... their life shall be like a watered garden, and they shall languish no more."

You will see a great exchange — "I will turn their mourning into joy; I will comfort them, and give them gladness for sorrow."

You will have a full and satisfied soul — "I will feast the soul of the priests with abundance, and my people shall be satisfied with my goodness, declares the Lord."

Think about that. *Each one of them that were shattered by oppression would have God personally attend to them and faithfully nourish them back to full strength.* They had a reason to hope.

I also want you to notice Jeremiah's response to these comforting truths. He believed that the promises were true and would be fulfilled, so Jeremiah awoke revitalized and re-energized — "At this I awoke and looked, and my sleep was pleasant to me" (Jer. 31:26). It may not happen as immediately as this but eventually what we believe about the goodness and providence of God has an impact on our levels of joy, peace and hope:

> *May the God of hope fill you with all joy and peace in*
> *believing, so that by the power of the Holy Spirit you may*
> *abound in hope. (Rom. 15:13)*

Such is the power of believing and internalizing the truth of God's words to us. When you really get it, *you begin to live in the benefit of that truth even before the fulfillment of the truth.* Even now, allow the promise of restoration to your soul to begin to lift and invigorate you. Allow God's ability to redeem you and ransom you to begin to increase your joy. The everlasting God will renew your strength.

If you tap into the resources that God has provided — *your tank will be full again.*

PART ONE:

IS IT WELL WITH YOUR SOUL?

CHAPTER ONE:
RUNNING ON EMPTY

Be gracious to me, O LORD, for I am languishing. (Ps. 6:2)

The day was full of promise. We were heading to the lake for the maiden voyage of my dad's boat. It would not be the biggest or newest boat on the lake, but the powerful engine promised hours of delight in the summer sun. Having never previously had access to a boat, we (my dad, his new bride and my family of five) had packed up excitedly.

On our list was sunscreen, food, drinks, life jackets, hats and fishing gear. We also packed a giant three-person inflatable tube that my boys would hang on to for dear life as we made laps around the lake. This would be a day to remember.

On arrival at the lake we launched the boat and began the party. I even went for a ride on the tube with my boys while grandpa ruthlessly carved figure-eights in the lake. I was so frightened I was mentally going over my life insurance coverage.

We were having a great time. We may have even begun to feel a bit smug that we were now legitimately lake people. Then it happened. The engine sputtered to a stop. We sat in the middle of the lake while Grandpa scrambled around the boat trouble-shooting every conceivable mechanical problem. Then his new bride asked the dreaded question, "Bill, did you remember to bring gasoline?!"

Now, no matter what age you are, no newlywed wants to ever hear that kind of question. Sheepishly, my dad admitted that we were out of fuel. The boat had two tanks, but in all of the excitement of the day he had forgotten to fuel up. "No problem", I said, "we'll just pull the boat back to shore."

I would live to regret that cavalier comment. For an hour and a half my boys and I strenuously pushed and pulled in the water while grandpa rowed with the singular paddle that was on board. The new bride was not happy and she reminded my dad of that fact periodically on the way back to shore. It was a long journey for him!

Finally, we reached the shore. You would be amazed at how exhausting that journey was! By the time we got back to shore we were not having fun anymore.

The boat had glided through the water swiftly and effortlessly when the engine had fuel in it, but when we were on empty everything moved in slow motion as we strained to get back safely to shore. I found through experience that the boat was not designed to be pulled by a rope in your teeth while you dog-paddle! When you are running on empty everything takes more effort and becomes less enjoyable.

You were not designed to run on empty.

It has not been easy for me to give myself and others permission to seek refuelling. Perhaps you too have resisted the idea that good-hearted, hard-working, faithful people need restoration of the soul. Yet the fact remains that we all need to remember to refuel in order to live the powerful, full lives that God intended us to live.

But many factors hold people back from seeking the refreshing that their heart needs, such as:

- *Busyness* — running constantly and not taking time for pit stops

- *Pride* — wishing to be viewed as being invincible

- *Hopelessness* — doubting that restoration is possible

- *Timidity* — being unduly concerned about burdening someone else to get help

- *Ignorance* — not understanding how to tap into the resources God has made available to us

- *Uncertainty* — being unsure of who can be trusted to speak to about matters of the soul

YOU ARE NOT ALONE

If you feel as though you need healing for the hurts and wounds that life inevitably brings our way, *you are in good company.* Many people in the Bible experienced exhaustion, frustration and emotional lows.

For example, Moses despaired at times as he carried out his divine assignment. He vented his anger and cried out in frustration to God when he felt he could no longer stomach the people God had given him to lead. Likewise, Elijah had obeyed God but his life was still in danger. As he fled his enemy he was so exhausted, terrorized and perplexed at how events had turned out that he also asked God to end his life. Similarly, Peter wept bitterly and uncontrollably after he had denied Christ three times. He hit a low point because of the distance between who he wanted to be and who he had become.

Additionally, in the Psalms we see people struggling with reconciling what they knew of the goodness of God with what was going on in their hearts. We see them vocalizing the ache that was in their soul because of barbed words and hateful actions towards them. We see them looking for relief from the pain that the choices of others had inflicted on them, not to mention the pain that they inflicted on themselves. The transparency and honesty of the Psalms encourages each of us to be vulnerably human.

It is OK to need replenishment.

THE DANGERS OF RUNNING ON EMPTY

If you run on empty, you are exposing yourself to many possible dangers. Have you ever felt that you may be getting so fatigued that your physical health may be suffering? Have you ever tried to lead on empty and compromised your own effectiveness? Have you been immobilized by despairing thoughts? Have you been living with a sense of being overwhelmed and feeling unable to keep pace with the demands on your life? Have you surprised yourself by how close your anger and frustration are to the surface? Are you obsessed with thoughts of escape?

It is a dangerous thing to run on empty.

Unfortunately, when we do so we often make destructive choices rather than turning to God and the means of replenishment He provides. God says through the prophet Jeremiah:

> *"For my people have committed two evils:*
> *they have forsaken me,*
> *the fountain of living waters,*
> *and hewed out cisterns for themselves,*
> *broken cisterns that can hold no water." (Jer. 2:13)*

When you are not accessing living waters *you will attempt to get what you need for your soul from a source that is an imitation — one that is certain to disappoint.* We all know the let-down that comes from "drinking from the wrong well" in search of life. We are only left with an even greater emptiness.

IT DOESN'T HAVE TO BE THIS WAY

It is possible to know when your tank is getting low so that you can take preventative measures. One of the greatest tools that we are given is our emotions. Our emotions are like the flashing lights on the dashboard of a car that tell you something is wrong and changes need to me made!

Whenever you experience a negative emotion (such as envy, bitterness, rage) that is your cue to stop, to re-think your perceptions, change your responses and take measures to ensure the health of your soul. Depending on your level of self-awareness, you are either very tuned in to when your dash lights are flashing or you may have someone in your life hoping that you start to recognize what is so clear to them and others around you!

Yes, you *do* need to refuel. This may come as a shock to you — but you are vulnerable to the same draining effects that affect everyone else! Typically, when we are young we regard ourselves as invincible. We carry within us a streak of idealism. We are even quite determined that we will not grow old (our parents made that mistake but we surely will evade it!). We mistakenly think that the resiliency of youth goes on forever.

Yesterday I texted a high school friend I hadn't seen for a while and asked him how he was doing. He texted back, "Feeling my age"! It usually takes some life experience to learn that *health, energy and a sense of well-being tend to get drained away over time and are only retained if you are intentional.* Your tank only stays full if you take measures to keep it full. I am sure that you have noticed how, over time, *the gap widens between those who were intentional about the care of their body, soul and spirit and those who were not* (just check your Facebook account for confirmation!).

Clearly, the choices we make in our lifestyle, attitude, spiritual life and relationships influence whether we will run out of energy *or* have enough in the tank to accomplish our most treasured goals. They determine whether we become fatalistic *or* we continue to reach for our God-given potential, whether we become a blamer *or* a person who is a pleasure to spend time with.

By now I am sure that you will agree with me that it is critical that you refuel. But before we look at how that happens, we need to first understand how our tanks get emptied in the first place. Having an endless water supply does us no good if we have gaping holes in our buckets! Let's look at some of the primary reasons that people find their reserves depleted.

QUESTIONS FOR REFLECTION AND DISCUSSION:

1. In this season of your life, can you identify with the phrase "running on empty"?

2. Why do you think it is hard for people to admit that they need refueling?

3. Do you have any recurring warning signals in your life that indicate you have a significant need to refuel?

CHAPTER TWO:
WHAT DRAINS YOUR TANK?

Oh LORD, you hear the desire of the afflicted; you will strengthen their heart; you will incline your ear. (Ps. 10:17)

Stressful life events wear you down. Certain experiences will bring you from a normal emotional state into a more extreme state of stress, fear, anxiety or anger. These are your *stressors*. Not only do they exhaust you in the moment, *they also have a cumulative effect.* Every human being only has so many reserves for dealing with the snowballing effect of stressors. It doesn't matter how exceptional we may think we are, high levels of stress over extended periods of time eventually take their toll.

You have to take the effects of stress seriously. Because of the way that we are made, strain in one area of our lives will spill over into other areas. For example, Kenneth Greenspan of New York's Presbyterian hospital claims that stress now contributes to 90% of all diseases[1].

This is why it is so important to stay replenished, which is essentially "strengthening ourselves in the Lord". *When we do this we will have enough reserves for these often uncontrollable and unforeseen stresses that life throws at us.*

---

1   *Making Life Rich Without Any Money,* by Phil Callaway (Eugene, OR: Harvest House, 1998), p. 20.

Take a moment to consider what your stressors or 'triggers' may be:

☐ Hurtful words spoken to you by others

☐ Feeling that your job or a source of income is in jeopardy

☐ Having your health threatened by a physical injury, chronic ailment or disease

☐ Being excluded socially or rejected

☐ Being placed in the position of 'referee' between two warring parties

☐ Being the victim of gossip, slander or defamation

☐ Being torn between the expectations of different people in your life — and knowing you cannot possibly please all of them

☐ Facing hostility towards you or those you love

☐ Making a vocational and/or geographical move

☐ Launching a new business or creative venture

☐ Dealing with betrayal from a spouse, family member or co-worker

☐ Incurring a financial loss from an investment gone bad or an emergency expense

☐ Experiencing a traumatic event such as being the victim of a crime, neglect or abuse

☐ Other: _____

Wow, just reading that list is enough to knock some wind out of your sails! But press on — you need to know where the danger areas are if you are going to plan to manage and overcome them.

I did not see it coming when *many of these stressors were about to converge on my life at one time.* I was a leader. I thought I was strong and that events that affected *others* could not affect *me.* I quickly discovered that I was not super-human and that stress is no respecter of persons! I found that the greater the intensity of stressors were in my life, the more desperate for relief I became. It was out of that journey of pain, discovery and recovery that this book was born.

I want to help you to *recognize stress factors in your life and to offset their cumulative draining effect in your life.*

One of the surprising realities about stress is that not only 'negative' events bring us stress — *but 'positive' events do as well!* Do not underestimate the stress that positive life changes also bring about in your life. When you make helpful and constructive life changes you are drawing deeper into your physical, mental and spiritual reserves. Take note of the impact that these changes have on you, so that you can extend grace to yourself and to those close to you.

For example, over the past year we as a family have had many exciting changes and adventures as I have ventured out into a new vocational pathway. All of the changes are positive, but even good changes require monitoring and appropriate replenishment strategies (more on that later). Some of the changes we faced included a major career move into speaking and consulting (as with many career changes it is more demanding, and rewarding, than I imagined!), moving into a home office (office work becomes more of a challenge when I hear echoing through the house comments like "I have no clean underwear left!") and travelling widely (though we thoroughly enjoy our time with people once we arrive at our destination, we often sarcastically joke about how 'glamorous' travelling is!).

I have also been continually challenged spiritually and I have faced a big learning curve technologically as we have launched several ministry and business initiatives.

Take a moment and consider the level of pressure you may be experiencing because of 'life change stressors' — *positive or negative* — and how adjusting to these changes may be affecting your health and relationships[2]:

STRESS TEST

Event	Scale of Impact	Check if this applies
Death of a spouse	100	
Divorce	73	
Marital separation	65	
Jail term	63	
Death of close family member	63	
Personal injury or illness	53	
Marriage	50	
Fired at work	47	
Marital reconciliation	45	
Retirement	45	
Change in health of family member	44	
Pregnancy	40	
Sex difficulties	39	
Gain of new family member	39	

---

2   This resource is available online at www.powertochange.com/life/stresstest

Business readjustment	*39*
Change in financial state	*38*
Death of close friend	*37*
Change to different line of work	*36*
Change in # of arguments with spouse	*35*
Mortgage over $200,000	*31*
Foreclosure of mortgage or loan	*30*
Change in responsibilities at work	*29*
Son or daughter leaving home	*29*
Trouble with in-laws	*29*
Outstanding personal achievement	*28*
Spouse begins or stops work	*26*
Begin or end school	*26*
Change in living conditions	*25*
Revision of personal habits	*24*
Trouble with boss	*23*
Change in work hours or conditions	*20*
Change in residence	*20*
Change in schools	*20*
Change in recreation	*19*
Change in church activities	*19*
Change in social activities	*18*
Large loan	*17*
Change in sleeping habits	*16*
Change in number of family gatherings	*15*
Change in eating habits	*15*
Vacation	*13*

Christmas	*12*
Minor violations of the law	*11*
	TOTAL

If your total score is under 150 you are less likely to be suffering the effects of cumulative stress, however any score over 100 should be given due concern. If it is between 150 and 300 you may be suffering from chronic stress, depending on how you perceived and coped with the particular life events that occurred. If your score is over 300 it is likely you are experiencing some detrimental effects of cumulative stress (note that the degree to which any particular event is stressful to you depends on how you perceive it).

THE PAIN DRAIN

Not only do we need to increase our awareness of how stressful events eat away at our reserves, but we also need to be aware of *how negative experiences from our family of origin can leave us with a greater vulnerability towards becoming depleted.*

My family of origin is colourful indeed. I do not want to go into a lot of detail, but just to assure you that I can speak to this area with authority, allow me to give you a brief snapshot. On my mother's side of the family there was deep trauma as a result of poverty, addictions and a lack of understanding of their value in the eyes of God. Without going into detail, there were many forms of abuse in the home that resulted in extensive emotional suffering for my mother in her formative years. Although I was quite young when most of this trauma came to the surface in my mom's life, I do remember some of it, and relatives have filled in some of the terrible details I did not remember. Even though my mom was a fun-loving lady, all that she had seen had taken its toll on her and the result was that she was in and out of institutions during my growing up years.

These types of experiences shape the kind of home life a child grows up in. I am only now beginning to recognize the power that unmet childhood needs have on a person in their later years. It can impede your ability to distinguish between people that are good for you or bad for you. It can influence you towards mimicking unproductive ways of coping with stress that were modelled for you. It can lead to patterns of thinking that are self-limiting and self-condemning. You may default to attempting to get from authority figures what you lacked from your parents. You may be driven to please others beyond healthy, sustainable levels.

I did not understand my own vulnerability until I encountered the stressful period of time that I referred to earlier. When I became overwhelmed by enormous pressures related to my work life, I began to appreciate that I was not immune to the effects of sustained stress on the human mind and body.

Any person that has had a less than stellar home life needs three things. First, you need a healing of the heart because of what you have experienced. Second, you need to re-examine the unhealthy patterns of thinking that you learned. Third, you need be freed of the false conclusions that you've drawn about yourself and replace them with the truth.

Thank God, my life dramatically changed at the age of fifteen when I submitted my life to the love and lordship of Jesus Christ. *Although God did not automatically sweep all of my problems away, I was given a solid foundation that had the potential to make me resilient no matter what I experienced.*

I see now that the greatest danger *is not in what happened to me but in what I believed as a result of what happened.* More on that in "Part Two", but for now I want to help you identify and recognize the impact that your developmental years had on your patterns of thinking. You may have not grown up in a safe family environment. You may have been expected to be perfect. You may have had damaging words spoken to you by authority figures. You may have experienced trauma.

Are you able to discern any destructive ways of thinking or faulty beliefs about yourself, others and God that you may have as a result? The results are more predictable than you think. People's reactions to present circumstances, especially when they are under pressure, often reveal the faulty coping mechanisms people picked up in their youth. But you can take heart! These stubborn patterns can be confronted and changed!

BATTLE WEARY

Another major depleting factor is the effects of living in a world that is both tainted by human sin and affected by demonic forces. Evil is real. We are at war. Everything that God loves is a potential target for Satan because he is jealous of the affection and loyalty that flows to God. This includes such areas as: the health of your church or organization, the fidelity of your marriage, your rapport with your colleagues and your overall well-being.

Satan's aim is to thwart God's purposes in your life and drain away the joy and full experience of life that Jesus wants you to have (John 10:10). In fact, *the areas in your life that carry the most potential for fulfillment and clout are the areas that most carefully need to be protected from the enemy's schemes.*

The reality of pure evil being active in the world is a difficult concept for many Westerners to grasp — even those who are 'churched'. It simply does not fit well with our material worldview. As a result, when searching for life solutions we tend to favour environmental, social and psychological factors and ignore the possibility of spiritual factors. In reality, *I expect all of these factors and more to be at play whenever we face a human problem!*

My point here, though, is to help you understand that you have been culturally conditioned to underestimate the threat of spiritual attack on you and what you love. *That puts you at a distinct disadvantage.* When the apostle Paul wrote to Christians to increase their awareness "the schemes of the devil", he did not say *if* an evil day comes but *when* the evil day would come (Eph. 6:11-13).

We must be prepared for the inevitable. Our awareness needs to be increased. When we fail to see the connection between our daily lives and spiritual realities we are susceptible to two common miscalculations.

First, *we fail to recognize the possibility of dark forces at work in human interactions*: "For we do not wrestle against flesh and blood, but against the rulers, against the authorities, against the cosmic powers over this present darkness, against the spiritual forces of evil in the heavenly places" (Eph. 6:12). This chapter teaches that, in the context of human relationships, you need to "arm yourself" by:

- Protecting how you think (the helmet of salvation)

- Being held together by truth (the belt of truth)

- Guarding yourself with right attitudes and actions (the breastplate of righteousness)

- Exercising your faith in order to block Satan's fiery missiles (the shield of faith)

- Remaining open to share with others the gospel of peace (feet ready with the gospel)

- Effectively wielding the word of God against lies that come your way (the sword of the Spirit).

Second, *we fail to recognize the gravity of not releasing anger and malice towards another person*: "Be angry and do not sin; do not let the sun go down on your anger, and give no opportunity to the devil" (Eph. 4:26-27). Anger that is not properly released and dealt with by the time you lay your head on the pillow becomes a breeding ground for bitterness and rage that corrodes the soul. When you are in this state of mind it gives Satan the opportunity to suggest ways of expressing your ill-will in dark ways — whether that be through lashing out (damaging the relationship) or internalizing the anger and isolating yourself (damaging your own well-being). We will look at how to release and forgive people in a later chapter.

Keep in mind that the teaching on spiritual warfare in Ephesians happens *in the context of human relationships.* Whenever you see that lies are being believed and causing strife within a relationship it is reasonable to consider that some type of warfare may be in play. The Bible clearly teaches that Satan is the 'father' or source of all lies. This is especially apparent when a situation begins to cause tormenting thoughts for those involved. For example, you could be 'walking on eggshells' around your spouse or a co-worker because of false assumptions you have about their perception of you or your behavior.

Jesus has already defeated Satan and equipped believers in Christ for all that they need to triumph over spiritual attack. *The scripture is clear about the delegated authority we have from Christ to deal decisively with demonic powers.* In Col. 1:13 we learn that believers are delivered from the authority of the kingdom of darkness. In James 4:7 we learn that believers need only resist the devil and he will flee from them. Finally, in Luke 10:19 we take comfort in the fact that Christ has given all believers authority over all the power of the enemy.

Much has already been written in this regard, therefore my goal here is to simply increase your awareness that spiritual battles can wear you down. Due diligence is required to keep your spiritual reservoir full to meet the challenge.

Are you battle weary? If so, I want you to know that every provision has been made for you! The apostle Peter wrote to Christians who had experienced suffering, some of which was initiated by their adversary the devil (1 Peter 5:8). Though it was painful at the time, they were given full assurance that God would grant them full recovery and restoration: "And after you have suffered a little while, the God of all grace, who has called you to his eternal glory in Christ, will himself *restore, confirm, strengthen* and *establish* you" (1 Peter 5:10, emphasis mine).

God himself takes a personal interest in your restoration and energizes the entire process. Each word in the original language would have given the original readers of this letter a nuanced understanding of the restoration process that they could anticipate in their lives[3]:

- *Restore.* God himself will set you right, mending and repairing what has gone wrong into appropriate condition so you will function well.

- *Confirm.* God himself will make you solid, giving you stability and sustaining you so you will be able to bear up under pressure.

- *Strengthen.* God himself will increase your capability, giving you grace to meet the demands of life.

- *Establish.* God himself will secure you, giving you a foundation that is permanent and unwavering.

I realize that this topic can seem very ethereal for many people, but I want you to know that *the battles are real and that God's counteracting provisions are practical indeed.* In each unique situation, Jesus has many 'real world' solutions to restore, confirm, strengthen and establish you.

To show you what this can look like, I recall a time in my life when the spiritual attacks I was experiencing were unprecedented. They took the form of a sense of spiritual heaviness, overwhelming people problems and accompanying tormenting thoughts. I had seen nothing like it before or since!

It was during that period of time that God began to *restore* me through such means as a weekly soaking time of prayer and

---

3   http://www.preceptaustin.org/1_peter_510-14.htm

worship that a few of us gathered for, as well as restorative people and events that I exposed myself to. God began to *confirm* me by having truth spoken into the situation from outside sources and even by giving me dreams that brought certain issues to light. God began to *strengthen* me by giving me affirmations from trusted godly people, by increasing my personal capacity and by helping me with truths from His Word and the works of trusted authors. God began to *establish* me by delivering me from the situation, bringing new helpful partnerships to me, expanding my networks and restoring my confidence. I found God's work of restoration to be both practical and progressive.

In this chapter we have covered a lot of ground. We have walked through the process of identifying a variety of possible draining effects in your life. In "Part Two" we will look more thoroughly at what to do about them. But before we go there, let's look at one more possible draining factor in your life: difficult people.

QUESTIONS FOR REFLECTION AND DISCUSSION:

1. How are your stress levels? Is your score from the above test what you thought it might be?

2. Do you feel like you have the inner reserves to handle stressful events/factors well right now, or that you are almost crumbling under pressure?

3. What are the biggest stressors in your life right now? Can any of these be eliminated or decreased by a change in your circumstances or relationships?

CHAPTER THREE:
WHO PULLED THE PLUG?

Though I walk in the midst of trouble, you preserve my life; you stretch out your hand against the wrath of my enemies, and your right hand delivers me. The LORD will fulfill his purpose for me; your steadfast love, O LORD, endures forever. (Ps. 138:7-8)

Of all of the possible draining influences in life, dealing with difficult people has to be near the top of the list! The level of drain on your life is in direct proportion to your exposure to people who are not good for you. Perhaps you too have run into people who have the spiritual gift of 'criticism'!

In my experience, Christians are particularly naïve about difficult people on several levels. We assume that everyone will want and respond positively to our good-hearted efforts to help them. We find it difficult to believe that truly misguided or destructive people may be part of the community. We drastically underestimate the negative influence of certain people. We wrongly assume that every person is equally worthy of the same level of trust, time and investment.

As a result, many people are stuck in relationships that are *life-draining* rather than *life-giving*. When it comes to people they associate with, they do not heed the warnings of Proverbs:

"The prudent sees danger and hides himself, but the simple go on and suffer for it." (Prov. 22:3)

"Keep your heart with all vigilance, for from it flow the springs of life." (Prov. 5:23)

They do not make efforts to "keep out the bad and let in the good"[4].

INTENTIONALITY IN RELATIONSHIPS

David Kraft lists five primary groups of people that we can choose to spend our time with[5]: resourceful people, important people, trainable people, nice people, and draining people. The first three are good for you and the last two are not. You become like those you spend time with, so you need to be slow and deliberate about the selections you make.

You want to prioritize spending time with *resourceful* people. They help you get to where you're going in life. They gladly share with you the knowledge, skills, ideas and networking connections that you need. You also want to prioritize *important* people, ensuring that you give quality time with friends, family, and mentors. Finally, you want to invest in *trainable* people whose willingness to learn makes them a candidate for mentoring and resourcing.

Why does Kraft warn his readers about the dangers of spending time with *nice* people? It seems quite counter-intuitive doesn't it? Well, imagine that you had a destination to get to but you never got there because you always spent time with people that were *nice*. They are pleasant enough company, but at the end of the day time with them ends up being a distraction that costs you a great deal. I

---

4   This is a helpful phrase that is repeated throughout *Boundaries,* by Cloud and Townsend (Grand Rapids: Zondervan, 1992).

5   David Kraft, *Leaders Who Last*, Crossway, Wheaton, IL . 2010, p. 130. Note that Kraft is writing particularly to leaders.

am sure that you have seen people make this misstep in life — they are forever spinning their wheels because none of the nice people in their inner circle have figured out how to get traction. Don't get me wrong — I like nice people and I like it when people are nice to me! Let me explain it this way — although we are called to love all people, *that doesn't mean that all people should have equal access to our time and energy.* There is limited space in your inner circle, so reserve those seats for your most valuable relationships!

And that fifth category of people is a pesky one, isn't it? *Draining* people are those who demand more of your time, and just as importantly, more of your mental energy than all of the other four combined! People may be draining for any number of reasons. In the end, it doesn't really matter *why* they are draining — what matters more is that you recognize *what is happening to you!* Good-hearted people tend to feel obligated to help everyone who is needy. However, if someone has a need, it doesn't necessarily mean that *you* are the one to meet it, that you are *able* to meet the need at this time, or that doing so would be the *best* stewardship of your energies.

THE WISE, THE FOOLISH, AND THE EVIL

Fortunately, we have in the book of Proverbs a treasury of wisdom for interpersonal relationships. This book of wise sayings was originally collected by Solomon (and other writers) for the purpose of imparting wisdom to sons that would inherit the throne. Thus, you see in virtually every chapter the writer urging his son to a wise course of action that will make him an effective leader.

Of course, Proverbs has relevance for every reader, but I draw this to your attention to let you know that a central concern of the writer(s) is *to ensure that the future king surrounds himself with people that are good for him.* The direction of the entire nation depends on the soundness of his choices in this regard. Specifically, the future king is to *avoid people who will be foolish and undermine his purpose, and to gather around him people that will be wise and help propel him forward in his God-given purpose.*

Thus, Solomon instructs his son to be discerning about who he allowed into his inner circle, for they will influence his formation and his decision-making processes by the direction of their own character and values. For example, he says, "Take away the wicked from the presence of the king, and his throne will be established in righteousness" (Prov. 25:5).

The reality is that people have a variety of intentions that need to be filtered through. It is not wise to think that all people have virtuous intentions when they are dealing with you, or you may be in danger of becoming a victim of an unsafe person. On the other hand, it is not healthy to become jaded and assume that no one has good-hearted intentions. Then you may be in danger of becoming an isolated individual incapable of receiving genuine help from others.

So, what does the process of discernment look like? Solomon provides tips that will help in discerning the difference between those that will be a constructive help and those that will prove to be a thorn in the side. As Henry Cloud is fond of saying, *the best predictor of future behaviour is past behaviour.* This is the key, Cloud says, to discerning whether a person is wise, foolish or evil[6].

INDICATIONS OF CHARACTER

First, *pay attention to their actions more than their claims:* "Many a man proclaims his own steadfast love, but a faithful man who can find?" (Prov. 20:6). Have you ever had someone declare their friendship and support the first time they met you, only to disappear after that? Over time, people's level of commitment to you is demonstrated. True friends and supporters are not fickle — they retain a long-term interest in your well-being. Demonstrated behaviours,

---

6   http://vimeo.com/43777476

not insistence with words, demonstrates the heart of the person (see also Prov. 26:23-26). Sometimes you have to just let people go when they claim loyalty but do not follow up.

Second, *the way they talk will tell you whether their influence will be positive or negative.* "Delivering you from the way of evil, from men of perverted speech" (Prov. 2:12). The Pulpit Commentary identifies this type of speech in the original as being untrustworthy because it frequently and wilfully distorts the truth. It comes from a spirit that is stubborn, scornful, self-willed, and rebellious. For example, they may distort the truth to their own advantage or they may call into question the most noble efforts of others.

Third, *their reaction to correction will tell you their true character.* "Do not reprove a scoffer, or he will hate you; reprove a wise man, and he will love you. Give instruction to a wise man, and he will be still wiser; teach a righteous man, and he will increase in learning" (Prov. 9:8-9). Have you noticed that some people respond quickly to suggestions and correction, while others are *very* hard to get through to? Do they react against constructive feedback even when it is done for their benefit or do they welcome the input? Are they teachable and willing to receive from those that are further along the path than they are? A wise person will welcome feedback, even if it initially makes them uncomfortable.

Fourth, *their propensity to speak or to listen reveals what they will be like relationally.* For example: "A fool takes no pleasure in understanding, but only in expressing his opinion" (Prov. 18:2). "If a wise man has an argument with a fool, the fool only rages and laughs, and there is no quiet" (Prov. 29:9). "A fool gives full vent to his spirit, but a wise man quietly holds it back" (Prov. 29:11).

Fifth, *the way they process anger reveals the effect they will have on others around them.* "A hot-tempered man stirs up strife, but he who is slow to anger quiets contention" (Prov. 15:18). Anger in and of itself is not bad. Anger serves a purpose in that it lets you know that something needs to be changed. However, unbridled anger that introduces strife into a family, a church or a business is hazardous.

Sixth, *the way they treat people will give you a 'green light' or a 'red light'*. "Whoever belittles his neighbour lacks sense, but a man of understanding remains silent" (Prov. 11:12). They will cause you to feel honoured or dishonoured, valued or diminished. Be attentive to this.

Finally, *their habits of keeping conflicts alive or making peace will tell you what to expect in the future.* They will either seek peace or they will collude with others to keep conflicts alive: "For lack of wood a fire goes out, and where there is no whisperer, quarrelling ceases. As charcoal to hot embers and wood to fire, so is a quarrelsome man for kindling strife" (Prov. 26:20-21). They will tend to their own business or they will escalate the tensions that are outside the realm of their responsibility: "Whoever meddles in a quarrel not his own is like one who takes a passing dog by the ears" (Prov. 26:17).

Every friend or relational connection has potential for great blessing in your life. However, every friendship will at some point also disappoint you. That is OK. *You are not looking for perfect friends, but for those whose influence on you is more positive than negative.* To borrow a financial term, I like to think in terms of 'net' influence. After you subtract the bad from the good is there anything left? What is the 'net' influence of key people around you at this stage of your life?

As you hone your skills in discernment, there is a good chance that you will find that you have been allowing the wrong people close to you. Then what do you do?

DEALING WITH DRAINING PEOPLE

Here are some things that the Bible encourages you to do in order to deal with difficult or draining people:

Limit your exposure. Give unsafe people a wide berth. "Leave the presence of a fool, for there you do not meet words of knowledge" (Prov. 14:7). "Do not enter the path of the wicked, and do not walk in the way of the evil. Avoid it; do not go on it; turn away from it and pass on" (Prov. 4:14-15). It is no accident that every book that teaches people how to get traction in areas of their lives they wish to change emphasizes getting distance from toxic people! Be kind to everyone, but do not give your best energies to everyone.

Ignore aggravating comments. "The prudent ignores an insult" (Prov. 12:16) . There are many vocational roles (i.e.- people-helping professions) or family situations where you are more likely to be exposed to insulting statements. There are many dangers in 'owning' those statements and allowing the anger to be expressed outwardly in a thoughtless reaction, or having it turned inwardly causing despair. "Good sense makes one slow to anger, and it is his glory to overlook an offense" (Prov. 19:11). Do not allow your thoughts to dwell on offenses.

The best way that I have found to do this is through 'the principle of displacement'. This is filling the mind with a steady barrage of "the good" so that "the bad" is displaced (in much the same way as water in a jug is displaced by rocks).

Allow people to 'own' their issues. Each person is responsible for their own action and the consequences they bring. "If you are wise, you are wise for yourself; if you scoff, you alone will bear it" (Prov. 9:12). Yes, the Bible does encourage us to help others, but it always does so with warnings of the inherent dangers of doing so, and it teaches us to set limits on the help we offer. For example, Jesus gave his time freely to those who were open and receptive but he drew clear boundaries and limits with those that displayed a hard, critical spirit.

Realize the benefits will outweigh costs. Often people are held in damaging relationships because they do not want to give up some perceived benefit in the relationship — even if the relationship leaves them in a deficit position. For example, a woman may stay in an abusive relationship because she is afraid of being alone or uncertain or uncertain of her financial future. "Better is a dinner of herbs where love is than a fattened ox and hatred with it" (Prov. 15:17). While it is difficult to pull back from an unhealthy, unbalanced or co-dependent relationship, I have found that when I do so that God provides what I need through a more positive and helpful relationship.

Get a support group. "Whoever isolates himself seeks his own desire; he breaks out against all sound judgment" (Prov. 18:1). Healing, protection, perspective and restoration are available when you surround yourself with supportive people. It takes a sustained effort to build a supportive network and social life around you, but a laugh with trusted friends fills your tank like nothing else!

Do not seek revenge or harbour ill wishes towards the person. "Do not say, 'I will repay evil'; wait for the LORD, and he will deliver you" (Prov. 20:22). Part of the deliverance of God is that you no longer need to invest mental energies in matters concerning the person, or with how God may or may not deal with them. I have found that as I release the ill-will that I feel towards others, my mind and time are freed to pursue important things that improve, rather than detract from, my life.

Set limits on the damaging effects of difficult people. "Whoever says to the wicked, 'You are in the right,' will be cursed by peoples... but those who rebuke the wicked will have delight, and a good blessing will come upon them" (Prov. 24:24-25). Don't make the mistake of allowing and protecting irresponsible, inconsiderate behaviour. On one occasion, after dealing for a couple of years with a particularly toxic person, I realized that lines needed to be drawn. I am generally a soft-spoken person, but it seemed that the problems may go on indefinitely if I did not limit the damage this person was having in my life as a leader. Finally, I said, "Go ahead and say everything that you need to say today, because after this we are NOT having this conversation again!" The person said their piece, then I offered some kind words and a hug (I don't know if I would recommend always trying to hug someone who is always upset with you but it seemed to make sense at the time!). The best part of the story- I never had to listen to their corrosive complaining again!

Do not fear them. "The fear of man lays a snare, but whoever trusts in the LORD is safe" (Prov. 29:25). Fearing the reactions of people leads to cowardice and an avoidance of making difficult yet beneficial decisions. This can lead to a compromise of your emotional health and even the health of your organization.

I remember a time when I was called upon to speak to a group of people that had a history of being unresponsive (and even hostile) towards those who spoke openly about unresolved issues in the group. During that season of my life, I was learning to confront issues that needed to be dealt with, rather than leaving a mess for someone to clean up later! Unfortunately, I also have a need to be liked so I was in a conundrum. Before the event, I felt almost nauseous as anticipated the harsh reactions on the faces of people in the group that had incited unrest in the past.

At that time, I was reading through the writings of the prophet Jeremiah. Interestingly, Jeremiah had also been sent with a message to a resistant people. As a communicator of truth, Jeremiah would pay a personal price. Still, God asked him to boldly say what needed to be said! In particular, God's instruction to Jeremiah was that he not be 'afraid of their faces'! In other words, he was not to be fearful in anticipation of their reactions. By adapting God's message to my intimidating circumstance, I was able to take courage and deliver my message without backing down or waivering.

Turn to God to receive what you did not receive from people. "Even my close friend in whom I trusted, who ate my bread, has lifted his heel against me" (Ps. 41:9). The image David uses here is of getting a surprise mule-kick from someone he trusted! When this happens he wisely turns to God to receive grace: "But you, O LORD, be gracious to me" (v. 10). This was habitual for David: "And David was greatly distressed, for the people spoke of stoning him, because all the people were bitter in soul, each for his sons and daughters. But David strengthened himself in the LORD his God." (1 Sam. 30:6).

Recognize that people offer varying levels of support. Even if you are on a God-appointed mission there are still, at times, people who choose to be contrary — "Now there happened to be a worthless man… (who) blew the trumpet and said, 'We have no portion in David, and we have no inheritance in the son of Jesse; every man to his tents, O Israel'" (2 Sam. 20:1). In fact, *when you study Bible you discover that every person who was on a God-given mission had to be resourceful and find ways to carry on in spite of resistant people!*

KEEPING YOUR COMPOSURE

In one of the most remarkable stories in the Bible, we see how David dealt with difficult people. David was facing the humiliation of having to leave the capital city after his own son staged a coup. As David was fleeing, a random man that was bitter towards David began to harass and curse him. Apparently, the man felt powerful when he saw someone else in a position of disadvantage that he could exploit. It was so bad that the mighty warrior Abishai could not contain himself any longer and offered to shut the man up — *for good.* David's answer to the offer is astonishing:

> *"It may be that the LORD will look on the wrong done*
> *to me, and that the LORD will repay me with good for*
> *his cursing today." So David and his men went on the*
> *road, while Shimei went along on the hillside opposite him*
> *and cursed as he went and threw stones at him and flung*
> *dust. And the king, and all the people who were with him,*
> *arrived weary at the Jordan. And there he refreshed himself.*
> *(2 Sam. 16:12-14)*

David's answer shows he knew that harbouring resentment and striking out in revenge was not the best course of action. Instead, he chose to be free of the negative effects of a draining person by entrusting the outcome to God, ignoring the insulter, being free of vindictiveness and taking responsibility for refreshing himself.

You can be increasingly free from the effects of draining people and access the means of recharging that God provides!

WHAT FILLS YOUR TANK AND WHAT DRAINS IT

You may relate to some of the draining influences that we have covered so far, or you may be thinking of other ones that are factors in your life at this stage. The things that drain and fill our tanks will have similarities and differences for each one of us. They will also vary at different stages of life. List your current draining influences and begin to think of the ways your tank is filled[7]:

Drains	Fills

In the next chapter we will discover how getting your tank filled is not only possible, it is *promised* by God and available to you daily!

---

7   Adapted from *Leading On Empty*, by Wayne Cordiero
      (Bloomington: Bethany House, 2009), p. 91.

QUESTIONS FOR REFLECTION AND DISCUSSION:

1. What are the greatest draining factors in your life right now?

2. Do you have draining people in your life right now? Prayerfully think of what steps you need to take to diminish or completely stop the draining effect they have on your life. It may help to write this down in your journal. Make this a matter of serious prayer until you see a breakthrough!

CHAPTER FOUR:
THE HOPE OF REPLENISHMENT

"His soul shall abide in well-being." (Psalm 25:13)

In providing some steps towards recovery, I in no way want to oversimplify the healing process or make it sound easier than it is in real life. In reality, achieving holistic health is a lifelong journey for all of us. We all have blissful seasons and tragic seasons in life. It is easy to get discouraged in the dark valleys and wonder if we will ever enjoy the mountain tops again.

On one occasion, when I was receiving some much needed refreshing at a seminar, God gave me a picture that gave me hope in my own personal journey. The picture was of a moving sidewalk, like what you see in airports. My kids and I always have fun on them. When I walk down a moving sidewalk I feel like a giant taking massive strides past crowds of weary travellers. It was as though God wanted me to know that I need to get on and walk on the path of restoration — and that He will be there accelerating the process forward even when I am tired. When we take the long view and stay on the path, there is hope! Although I could not see it at the time, I am now enjoying the momentum and cumulative benefits that come from getting on a path towards recovery.

SHAKE IT OFF AND STEP UP!

I heard a story in a talk from Craig Groeschel at a Global Leadership Summit about overcoming adversity. This will bolster your determination and give you hope:

> A farmer owned an old donkey. One day, the donkey fell into the farmer's well. The farmer heard the donkey braying loudly and followed the sound to its source — and found the donkey standing at the bottom of the well.
>
> After carefully assessing the situation, the farmer sympathized with the old donkey, but the well was deep, and there was no way to haul the donkey out of it. The farmer called his neighbours, and asked them to come give him a hand — and to bring shovels.
>
> The neighbouring farmers came, with dirt and shovels in their trucks. Neither the donkey nor the well was worth the trouble of saving. The only thing they could think to do was to bury the old donkey in the well and put him out of his misery. It was a shame, but there was nothing else that could be done.
>
> As the farmer's shovelled dirt into the well, the old donkey was hysterical! The donkey brayed louder than ever when the dirt hit his back, but the farmers kept shovelling.
>
> Every time a shovel load of dirt landed on the donkey's back, he brayed loudly — but then he would shake it off and step up!
>
> As the dirt was shovelled down on top of him, the donkey continued. It became a rhythm — the farmers would drop a shovel load of dirt down the well, and the donkey would shake it off and step up. No matter how heavy the dirt, or

how distressing the situation seemed, the old donkey fought panic and just kept right on shaking it off and stepping up!

Finally, battered and exhausted, the old donkey stepped triumphantly over the edge of the well!

What seemed like it would bury him actually helped him... all because of the manner in which he handled his adversity. Instead of letting it bury him, the dirt became his road to freedom.

That's life! If we face our problems and respond to them positively, and refuse to give in to panic, bitterness, or self-pity, then the adversities that seem likely to bury us have within them the very real potential to help us. When loads of dirt are being dumped on you, just think: are you letting it bury you, or are you using it to climb upwards? Shake it off and step up![8]

Whatever the source of irritation and pain in our lives, what carries us through is our confidence that all of the good and bad in our lives can be used by God to accomplish his good purposes in our lives. He can give you the composure to "shake it off and step up"!

Sarah Young expresses this eloquently (writing with Jesus speaking in the first person):

Everything you endure can be put to good use by allowing it to train you in trusting Me. This is how you foil the works of evil, growing in grace through the very adversity that was meant to harm you. Joseph was a prime example of this divine reversal, declaring to his brothers: "You meant evil

---

8   This version of the fable is adapted from: http://rfhadley.com/shakeoff.htm

*against me, but God meant it for good."… Fear no evil, for
I can bring good out of every situation you will encounter.*[9]

PROMISES OF REPLENISHMENT

We have seen that tiredness, trauma, and heartache deplete the soul.
None of us are immune. Human beings are created in such a way
that stress and strain will eventually take their toll. We all get beat
up by events that life throws at us. The good news is that *God's plan
for us includes the healing of our hearts and the restoration of our souls.*
God cares about your total health. He has made every provision
for you to have a full tank!

When David's soul was overwhelmed, he took comfort in the
nature of God. He reminded himself that God is good and that
he is interested in restoring souls. Many truths in Psalm 23 sustained him:

> *The Lord is my shepherd; I shall not want.*
> *He makes me lie down in green pastures.*
> *He leads me beside still waters.*
> *He restores my soul.*
> *He leads me in paths of righteousness*
> *for his name's sake.*
>
> *Even though I walk through the valley of the shadow of
> death,*
> *I will fear no evil,*
> *for you are with me;*
> *your rod and your staff,*
> *they comfort me.*

---

9   *Jesus Calling*, by Sarah Young (Nashville, Thomas Nelson, 2004),
p. 134.

> *You prepare a table before me*
> *in the presence of my enemies;*
> *you anoint my head with oil;*
> *my cup overflows.*
> *Surely goodness and mercy shall follow me*
> *all the days of my life,*
> *and I shall dwell in the house of the Lord*
> *forever.*

David knew that God's restoration plan for his life was an "all-inclusive" package — it would include everything that his soul needed. *God, as his shepherd, provided constant oversight and care.* David needed to remind himself that God was for him. God's presence was more real than the loneliness he felt. He had the architect of the universe watching out for him, putting limits on evil in his life and ensuring a good ending to his life's story.

God provided rest and nourishment. He would have times when what he needed more than anything was some peaceful rest and bodily replenishment. He reminded himself that what he most needed, God most happily provided.

God provided guidance into what was good for him and protection from what was not good for him. The world, though at times replete with danger, could be navigated with the wisdom and insight he would receive from God.

God provided deliverance from fear. Sometimes the effects of carrying fear are more dangerous to us than the object of fear itself! In Psalm 34:4 David said, "I sought the Lord, and he answered me and delivered me *from all my fears*" (emphasis mine). Often what our soul requires, even more than a dramatic change of circumstances, is to be delivered from the corroding effects of fear. David was trusting God to bring him such calmness and confidence in his soul that he could heartily enjoy a feast even while enemies were in the vicinity. He knew that he did not necessarily need the removal of his object of fear — he needed the removal of fear from his heart. When fear was adequately subdued, he no longer needed to have an agitated soul.

God provided with extravagant generosity. David reminded himself of all of the abundance and overflow of God's riches towards him. When he thought of it, he realized that God took very good care of him, so much so that he had excess left over. We see him 'counting his blessings' in this Psalm — a spiritual discipline that served him well. David was intentional about reminding himself of the big-heartedness of God towards him, and *that led him out of self-pity and into praise.* An example of this is Psalm 103:1-5, "Bless the LORD, O my soul, and all that is within me, bless his holy name! Bless the LORD, O my soul, and forget not all his benefits, who forgives all your iniquity, who heals all your diseases, who redeems your life from the pit, who crowns you with steadfast love and mercy, who satisfies you with good so that your youth is renewed like the eagle's."

God provided His goodness and mercy. David reminded himself that, although at times he felt his needs and deficiencies acutely, it was in the nature of God to sweeten his journey along the way. David remains convinced of *the goodness of God.* The starting point for an effective replenishment strategy is to open ourselves to the hopeful possibility that God is good and kind. *He is able to weave everything in our life experience together for our good, for the good of others and for his glory.* For David there is hope because he is certain that the goodness of God remains a reality in spite of what his feelings are telling him in the moment. To reinforce the process he writes this song and confesses the truth out loud! In fact, he becomes so convinced of the care of God that he says that "goodness and mercy *shall follow me* all the days of my life" (v. 6 — *emphasis mine*). He is confident that if he waits long enough he will be overtaken by goodness. The very act of calling this truth to mind begins to restore the broken pieces of his soul. Meditating on the character of God has brought order into his inner world. In anticipation of the goodness coming his way in the future he has a reason to smile in the present.

God has provided eternal hope. Life in a broken world would inevitably carry its disappointments, but his soul would abide in well-being with the knowledge that he would dwell with God forever. Because the last chapter of his existence would be pure, uninterrupted and eternal fellowship with God, he would have joy and hope to sustain him in the current chapter of his life. This is a lost art today and something that we need to recapture from the saints that have gone before us. Learn to let the joy of your coming reward and the ecstasy of being in God's presence trickle back into the present, putting a song of praise on your lips and a lightness in your step. Savouring what will one day be yours gives you elation and endurance in the present.

I have included a list of additional promises of replenishment in the appendix that that will fill your tank (Resource Two: Replenishment Verses). These are verses that have substantially filled my tank and they are pulled directly from my quiet times with God. Here are a couple of them to whet your appetite:

> *This is my comfort in affliction, that your promise gives me life. (Ps. 119:50)*

> *The righteous flourish like the palm tree and grow like a cedar in Lebanon. They are planted in the house of the LORD; they flourish in the courts of our God. They still bear fruit in old age; they are ever full of sap and green. (Ps. 92:12-14)*

The Almighty amply provides for the needs of our souls through many avenues. Theologians have long referred to these avenues as "means of grace". I would describe the means of grace in the broadest sense possible and include *any and every means that God may use to strengthen your soul and energize your mission.* Through the many means of grace available to us, we actively position ourselves for His redeeming work in our lives. They are the keys in your strategy for revitalization.

In "Part Two" we will survey the means of grace that I have found to be the most beneficial in my journey as a follower of Christ. While all of them are essential, you will want to identify the ones that you particularly need to focus on in this season of your life. *The more your body, soul and spirit have been depleted, the more aggressive your replenishment strategy will need to be.* If you are not already on a pathway towards replenishment, it is time to get started!

GETTING ON THE PATH TO REPLENISHMENT

I had many opportunities to enjoy sports as a youngster. Some of my best days growing up were spent playing basketball, football or hockey — but nowhere did I spend more time than on the baseball diamond. I never did get a major league contract, which is too bad because pro baseball players live a soft life from what I can see! Sometimes they have to slide and get their pants dirty. Then they have to call a time-out and brush the dirt off. It doesn't strike me as the kind of work that should draw a multi-million dollar salary. But I digress.

One thing that players and fans of the game will tell you is that the best fielders are those who get the quickest 'jump' on the ball when it comes off the bat. In the instant that the ball bounces off the bat they are already off running — not in the direction of where the ball is, but where it is going. Players like this can make what might have been a hit for a double into what looks like a routine fly-ball. They are watching the pitch, the batter's stance, the speed of the swing and the angle that the ball comes off the bat. When they are observant, the location of the hit becomes predictable. And this really is why players need to get as many 'reps' in as possible in practice. Over time the arc and destination of a hit becomes increasingly foreseeable.

If you look honestly at the direction of your life, how is the trajectory looking? Can you sustain the pace you are currently living at? Are you going to have enough in the tank to make progress in the most important areas of your life? The great thing about understanding trajectory is that it gives you the ability to see where you are headed — *before you actually get there.*

The Bible word for this kind of wisdom is "prudence". Exercising prudence can save you a lot of pain in life. When you are prudent you see you are headed towards danger so you make a mid-course correction to avoid it.

> *"The prudent see danger and take refuge, but the simple keep going and pay the penalty." Prov. 22:3*

Oftentimes pain can be avoided when you learn to anticipate that grief is ahead on the route you have chosen! How many toxic relationships could be avoided? How many payments on depreciating items could be avoided? How many life-sucking jobs or contracts could be avoided? You get the picture. Often Pain can be avoided- and I want to get better at avoiding it (at the very least I do not want to walk into more pain than I need to!).

But what if your perception is off? Our perception can be blurred by pride, denial or even wishful thinking. It takes brutal honesty to have a clear perception of where our attitudes, choices and habits are taking us.

I remember a time when my perception was off. I had just revived my slo-pitch career. Well, there really is no such thing as a slo-pitch career. How can it be called a career when they call the league a 'beer league' and the pitcher lobs the ball at 10 miles per hour? Anyways, after having been out of the game for a number of years I was playing some decent ball and was asked to play for a higher division team. I was becoming a legend (in my own mind). No problem, I'll go out there and teach the young punks a lesson, I thought.

There really was a problem, though, because this was going to be my first night game. On top of that, it was drizzling. I was out in left field. Good move I thought — put your best outfielder in left field where he can really shine. Everything was fine until a routine fly ball came my way. I followed the arc of the ball but to my surprise, and embarrassment, I totally missed it. I must have looked like an angry camper swatting at a mosquito. I didn't even come close. Then another ball came my way and I totally missed again. I could have fielded the ball better when I was 7 years old. What had happened?

For the first time in my life I needed eye-glasses. Somehow the combination of playing under lights and the rain had brought this realization to me.

I wonder how many people are walking around thinking, "I'm seeing everything in my life accurately. I'm not in any danger. I am sustainable. Other people will fall short of their goals but not me. I'm not heading in the direction of pain." All the while they are not seeing that the direction of critical aspects of their lives is clearly off course. *I'm asking you to be brutally honest with yourself.* Are you truly on a path towards continual replenishment?

I hope that this book helps you see the reality of the trajectory of your life more clearly so you can ensure that your tank is always getting 'topped up'. The truth is, we will learn either through prudence and wisdom or through the pain of consequences. Wisdom equals becoming better at early prediction.

Too many times I've gone further than I need to down a painful road before realizing where the road was going to end, both in my personal and professional life. Don't wait until a key relationship in our life breaks down or you lose your health before you apply wisdom to your life. One of the most important things you can do in life is to take the time to reflect deeply on where your replenishment choices, habits and practices are taking you.

RIGHT PATH = RIGHT DESTINATION

It is a hard thing for a man to admit that he has gotten lost. I could just say that I was sight-seeing, but if I would have just been sight seeing I wouldn't have been so upset when we lost our guide vehicle in downtown Budapest. I wouldn't have been so upset that I was headed into the downtown core where there was an all night rave beginning. Nor would I have been so upset that I was there with no GPS, no cell phone, no maps and no understanding of Hungarian beyond 'Hello'. I also would not have felt so responsible for the protection of my wife, who didn't appreciate the fact that I was lost. And I wouldn't have been stressed about getting the three teenaged girls that were part of our mission team back to the Operation Mobilization base, which was about 45 minutes out of the city.

My only problem was that I didn't know what direction from the city to go or what road to take. We tried getting directions at a convenience store, but that didn't go so well. Imagine an agitated foreigner pointing randomly at maps and street signs saying '*Hello*' over and over again. Somehow that didn't translate.

Finally we attempted to get out of the city in hopes of finding our way back to the base. At first I was hopeful when we got out of the city and I began to recognize a word on highway signs. I felt that I was on course because I saw a word that was familiar. As it turned out, the word just meant 'exit' in Hungarian — so that wasn't very helpful either.

And then I saw the large sign lit up above the freeway — Vienna, Austria 225 km's! We knew that was definitely not the destination we were aiming for so we got off the freeway. Amazingly, four hours later we were able to make our way back to the base — much to our relief and the relief of the teens' parents who were waiting at the base.

I don't recommend taking this random approach to getting to a destination in Eastern Europe. It was stressful. *Yet I am amazed* at how many times I have taken a haphazard approach to friendships, finances and free time.

The path that we are on will take us to a *predictable* destination. You are not special if you arrive at your desired destination — you just got on the right path and stayed on the right path long enough to see results. *The promises of God for your replenishment are yours for the taking, but you need to intentionally arrange your life so that you can access and benefit from them.* That, my friend, is the focus of "Part Two".

QUESTIONS FOR REFLECTION AND DISCUSSION:

1. Prayerfully read through the replenishment verses in the appendix (Resource Two: Replenishment Verses).

2. What is one truth or promise from God's word that can sustain you in this season of life?

3. Imagine how your life will look 5 years from now if you stay on the trajectory that you are on. How will your relationships at home and work look? Will you have great friendships? What will your financial situation look like? Will you be enjoying your work or just plodding? How about the health of your soul, spirit and body?

PART TWO:

PLANNING FOR REPLENISHMENT

CHAPTER FIVE:
RENEWING YOUR MIND

"Be transformed by the renewal of your mind." (Rom. 12:2)

In his book titled *Can You Hear Me?* Brad Jersak explains that what often damages us more than a troubling life event, are the *lies that are attached to that event.* For example, even if a child is abandoned, they can go on to have a rich and rewarding family life as they embrace their adopted family. However, if as a result of their birth parents' actions, they believe that they are unlovable, then they will go through life emotionally disabled.

The lies that we believe about ourselves, about God, and about others wreak havoc in our lives. Believing lies can lead to a diminished self-identity and sense of self-worth, depression and fear-induced immobilization. Believing lies can lead into the trap of resentment, social isolation and marital tensions. When we believe lies our faith, our financial well-being and our physical health can be compromised.

To receive healing we first need to discern the lies that we have accepted (very often as a result of damaging events in our lives). When we have identified the lie, we can then go to Jesus and open ourselves to what he says about the experience and about us. I like to call this experience "being washed in the truth".

Allow me to give you an example of how this has worked in my life. I once took a management position with an organization that had a complex staffing situation. A woman that had been previously hired was not willing to "play nice" with others on the team and brought toxicity to the environment. I knew I had to deal with the situation with integrity, rather than sweeping matters under the carpet, but the series of events that ensued ended up leaving me concerned for my own health. These included unfounded accusations levelled against me in retaliation, attempts by other managers to protect toxic people, breaches of confidentiality and by-passing organizational lines of authority.

During this time I became paralyzed by lies like these: that Christians should always be 'nice' and never confront, that God would not be able to bring me through the valley and that the outcome of this scenario would be mainly negative and impossible to ever recover from completely.

I felt trapped. I was unsure of whom I could trust. Even taking a holiday could not relieve the mental pressure I was living under. I had to direct extensive energy into correcting the lies that kept me oppressed. She was, like Naomi in the book of Ruth, in danger of allowing her painful circumstances to form her identity (Ruth 1:20).

One of the key moments in the process of becoming free was when I attended a Living Free conference at our friend's church. This church was especially strong in the area of helping people be healed from traumatic life events and damaging patterns of thought. It was here that I began to identify the lies that were binding me — and the way the truth would set me free. I was going to learn a simple, yet crucial, process for expunging lies from my life and replacing them with the truths of God's word.

Though we did not know it at the time, one of the resource people that had been brought into the conference was Dr. Ken Smylie, who directs a prayer ministry in Florida. We had previously felt that we would benefit from this ministry (not to mention the Florida sun) so we had hoped to visit him there. To our surprise he was present at the conference — *and* we were informed by a friend that he had an opening for a session with us!

To show you what the process looks like, the conversation went something like this:

Ken: How can I help? What is troubling you?

Me: I am having some tough challenges with a tough leadership situation.

Ken: What is the lie that you believe that is causing you to feel upset?

Me: I suppose I feel powerless because of people I am dealing with who seem to have a great amount of power. I'm intimidated. feel that I will not be able to recover from people disagreeing with me and not liking me.

Ken: What you need to do is renounce the lies that you have believed, and then follow that by receiving the Scriptural truths that counteract those lies.

Me: OK. I renounce the lie that people have power over me or that they can control me. Yes, I renounce the lie that I need to be paralyzed by fear of them. I receive the truths that God is *bigger* than anyone who comes against me, that I am entirely secure in Christ and that He is with me. *Nothing and no one can thwart God's purpose for me.*

Ken: Do you receive that truth?

Me: Yes.

Ken: Then it is yours! I affirm the truth that God is with you, that He strengthens those who seek to please him and that He makes His faithfulness known *especially* in times of need. Rob, there is a spiritual battle here (at this point he smiles a broad smile), but Jesus loves a good fight! How do you feel?

Me: I feel 'lighter' and less anxious.

That conversation shows us the crucial steps in the process of understanding what it means to *renew my mind*. But I knew that this was just the beginning. I made it a goal — no, an obsession — to work daily at countering the lies that were drowning me.

Since then have I mined the Bible for every possible truth that may be the key to my freedom! I needed to immerse myself in truth.

THE TRUTH WILL SET YOU FREE

Whenever I have begun to waiver, these essential truths about God have helped me to regain my equilibrium:

1. God is absolutely good

One of the first possible casualties when you go through a period of intense trial can be your confidence that God is good and that He has your best interests in mind. I remember the first time in my Christian experience I began to question my faith. Fortunately, I realized that *I was associating imperfect reflections of God (broken people), with God Himself.* God's perfect holiness and overflowing compassion had not changed — what had changed was my perception of Him. In actuality He had always remained entirely trustworthy, just and good.

> *"For he is good, his steadfast love endures forever." (2 Chron. 5:13)*

> *"Let your saints rejoice in your goodness." (2 Chron. 6:41)*

2. God sees your affliction

Hagar, a servant of Abram and Sarai, had been sent away because of Sarai's contempt for her. After being treated harshly, she felt she was forgotten by God. She was pregnant and fleeing from her mistress. In the wilderness "the angel of the LORD *found* her" (Gen. 16:7, emphasis mine) — this tells us that God *pursues* those who are marginalized, rejected and scorned. She thought that she was beyond the scope of God's care — but nothing could be further from the truth. After God appeared to her and spoke to her she exclaimed, "You are a God of seeing… Truly I have seen him who looks after me" (Gen. 16:13). She named the well where God met her "the well of the Living One who sees me".

3. God is present

Jacob thought that he would only get ahead in life by the force of his own actions. En route to finding a wife and giving his angry brother time to cool off, God spoke promises to him in a dream, telling him that he would inherit the land that he was journeying through. When he awoke he said, "Surely the LORD is in this place, and I did not know it." He called that place "the gate of heaven" (Gen. 28:16, 17). In other words, he had perceived God as being *absent*, but in actuality God was *present and active, revealing and speaking, promising and guiding*. Jacob's awareness of God had increased so much that he in essence called the place a 'portal' to heaven — a unique space where the lines were blurred between his ordinary existence and the realm of the splendour of God!

4. God is redeemer

When David had someone proudly announce to him that they had helped to eliminate Saul, he stood aghast. He explained that he didn't need them taking action on his behalf because it was God who worked on his behalf. David had seen the sovereignty of God at work: "As the LORD lives who has redeemed my life out of every adversity…" (2 Sam. 4:9). He had seen that God had the ability to intervene in every danger he faced, so he had full confidence that God could re-purpose and orchestrate adverse circumstances so that he ultimately triumphed. He trusted God as his redeemer. The adversity was real, yet in every situation the Lord got personally involved and liberated him.

5. God's plan for your life prevails

God has a plan, and though opposing forces work to frustrate the plan, God does not allow his purpose to be thwarted. This truth held Job together after all that he had been through. He confessed: "no purpose of yours can be thwarted" (Job 42:2) and "He will complete what He appoints for me" (Job 23:14). In fact, God is so powerful and good that he can even do this, through turning the negative intentions of others for our good! "Instead the LORD your God turned the curse into a blessing for you, because the LORD your God loved you." (Deut. 23:6)

6. God is just

Too often we take on the weight of thinking that every injustice is our job to correct. That is God's job. He takes note of the actions of people and will ultimately hold them accountable. How He does that is his business, *not mine.* David gets this. When he was being unjustly hunted by Saul, *he relaxed in God's capable hands rather than taking matters into his own hands* (1 Sam. 24 "may the LORD judge between me and you"). He had learned to allow consequences and the actions of God to take their course rather than burdening himself with thoughts of revenge.

When we grasp all of these truths about God's good intentions for us, our spirits are lifted. One example of this was Hannah, who was in "great anxiety and vexation" because she had been "provoked" and "irritated" by her rival. When the priest Eli assured her that her prayers of distress had been answered she believed what he said. As a result of receiving that word of promise "her face was no longer sad" (I Sam. 1:18). This powerfully demonstrates how our beliefs about God affect our emotional state and even our countenance!

THY WORD IS A LIGHT UNTO MY PATH

So critical is the need to be guided by truth that Israelite kings *were required to physically transcribe their own personal copy of the Word of God and review it daily.* This would have been a painstaking process, but one that helped them get intimately familiar with each truth that they needed to fulfill their God-given destiny. The result? He would rule well and be successful because of the reverence, humility and focus this would cultivate in his life:

> *"And when he sits on the throne of his kingdom, he shall write for himself in a book a copy of this law, approved by the Levitical priests. And it shall be with him, and he shall read in it all the days of his life, that he may learn to fear the LORD his God by keeping all the words of this law and these statutes, and doing them, that his heart may not be lifted up above his brothers, and that he may not turn aside from the commandment either to the right hand or to the left, so that he may continue long in his kingdom, he and his children, in Israel". (Deut. 17:18-20)*

In addition to having a time daily in the word of God, I encourage you to absorb as much as you can from trusted sources that will help you understand how God has wired you and how you can stay encouraged and motivated in your life mission. Whether as a measure of recovery or to simply take a preventative measure, I strongly believe that every person needs to take daily steps towards mental and emotional health. Read books, listen to podcasts and seek out experiences that offset negative influences in your life. Authors that have energized me the most lately — to name a few — have been Dan Miller, Henry Cloud and Sandi Krakowski. You need to proactively put tools into your hands and learn the skills, mindsets and processes that you need to adopt in order to live a more peaceful and joyful existence.

A crucial key in this process is the practice of *filtering your problems through truth*. This is how Mordecai mentored and instructed his niece Esther when their people faced the imminent threat of ethnic cleansing: *"And who knows whether you may have not come to the kingdom for such as time as this?" (Esther 4:14)*. Every great victory in Scripture happened when people saw a challenge as an opportunity for God to leverage the position they were in.

Amazing possibilities will open up when you focus on the truth of who God is and what he can do rather than on the obstacles you are faced with!

GETTING ROUGH WITH SELF-PITY

One of the biggest hindrances to being set free by truth is a mindset of victimization and self-pity. When you feel your soul sliding in that direction, you need to recognize how dangerous it is. If you get into a "woe is me" attitude, everything that you hold dear is placed in jeopardy- your health, your net worth, and your relationships. To get unstuck you need to *take responsibility for the orientation of your own soul, confront your emotions* and *chose to hope and trust in God.* This is what the Psalmist did in Psalm 42:5-6:

> *Why are you cast down, O my soul,*
> *and why are you in turmoil within me?*
> *Hope in God; for I shall again praise him,*
> *my salvation and my God.*

This blog post wonderfully demonstrates this process in a somewhat humorous and transparent way!

Take Every Thought Captive[10]

One of my favourite verses is 2 Corinthians 10:5, where Paul instructs us to "take captive every thought to make it obedient to Christ."

I love the way that's phrased in the NIV. I picture myself on a horse with a lasso, wrangling rogue thoughts, tying them up and then whipping them into shape.

Grabbing "I'm An Idiot" by the neck and pounding on it until it becomes "I Am God's Child."

---

10   http://messionaryme.wordpress.com/2012/12/

Got to get rough with those negative thoughts. They're a wild bunch. Horns and everything.

And Saturday, they were on a stampede.

I'd had a lovely brunch with three new friends. I left feeling lifted up, praising God for amazing fellowship.

But within 30 minutes, my self-doubt unleashed a herd of ugly:

I said all the wrong things.

I jeopardized the conversation.

I revealed too much, too soon.

Those girls don't really like me.

I needed to go lay face down on my closet floor in prayer, flood my brain with God's truth until those lies were drowned...

Enough.

Several years ago, a dear friend organized a study of Beth Moore's Breaking Free. On the last day, to encourage us in what we had learned, she gave each member of the group a set of spiral bound index cards. She called them "truth cards." Her intent is that we would fill the cards with God's truth from scripture, so we'd have a quick reference to hit when Satan's lies attempted to put us back in chains.

The first verse I wrote on my truth cards was Galatians 5:1:

"It is for freedom that Christ has set us free. Stand firm, then, and do not be burdened by a yoke of slavery."

Saturday night, that verse powered my lasso. It filled me with righteous rage, fuelling my attack against my own brain.

How dare I allow myself to become slave to lies, when Christ died to give me freedom in my Saviour's arms?

How dare I allow Satan to undo in my head what Jesus has done in my heart?

I love Jesus too much to let his truth be overrun by a lack of confidence in Him.

So one by one, I rounded up every thought.

And by the power and grace of God, I turned each to truth:

I am fearfully and wonderfully made.

I am worth dying for.

Nothing can separate me from the love of Christ! This story illustrates how misbeliefs are often our greatest enemies. They are the culprits behind many of our problems that drain us, including: anger, anxiety, depression and perfectionism. We also see that increasing freedom from distorted self-talk is possible, by learning to challenge your internal dialogue with reality and biblical truth. Set yourself on a course of truth therapy today!

QUESTIONS FOR REFLECTION AND DISCUSSION:

1. What are some of the recurring lies that you've bought into about yourself and your life?

2. How have these lies and habits of wrong thinking affected your relationships and sense of well-being, as well as your ability to fulfill your calling?

3. What are God's truths that counter each of these lies? Write them down.

4. What kind of steps do you need to take to be transformed by the renewing of your mind? What is your replenishment strategy in this area?

CHAPTER SIX:
FORGIVING YOUR DEBTORS

Do not repay evil for evil or reviling for reviling but on the contrary, bless;
for to this you were called, that you may obtain a blessing. For "Whoever
desires to love life and see good days, let him keep his tongue from evil and
his lips from speaking deceit; let him turn away from evil and do good; let
him seek peace and pursue it." (1 Peter 3:9-11)

Harbouring hatred towards others is perhaps the most toxic decision a person can make. We don't like to talk about forgiveness
because we would rather nurse our grudge against the person
who offended us. It offends our sense of justice that they would be
acquitted for their crime against us.

But forgiveness does not let the other person 'off the hook' in
the sense of ignoring the reality that we have been sinned against.
When we forgive, we acknowledge that the person's actions
towards us were wrong and that injury was done to us — however,
we are releasing them from their debt. We are releasing ourselves of
the desire to make them pay for their sin against us. We are leaving
them in the hands of God for Him to deal with as He wills. We are
walking away free from the bitterness that rots our souls.

When we refuse to forgive and release, our lives remain
enmeshed with people who are not good for us. Why would we
stay in emotional bondage to them?

Unforgiveness puts the other person in a position of control in your life and it holds you in a perpetual state of being a victim. You feel powerless. You feel stuck. You are miserable. You have trouble moving on from that point. Someone else bullied you or took advantage of you but you are keeping them in a position of power over you because you retain the wound. You allow their position of power over you to erode your self-image and confidence. You allow the other person to be in the driver's seat of your life.

Forgiveness, on the other hand, empowers you because *you are making a choice independently of the perpetrator.* Your well-being is no longer *conditional* on what they do or do not do — or even on whether they ever apologize or not. You are making a choice for your well-being that no one can stop. You are choosing to no longer be a victim. You are choosing to move on and pursue God's best for your life. You are in the driver's seat of your own life again. You become free in the truest sense of the word!

But the problem is that retaining our resentment *makes so much sense to us at the time.* We think this will ensure that someone will take notice and take our side in the matter — but this keeps you in a victim mentality. We think this will punish the offender and make certain they are corrected and brought to justice, but some people *waste years and decades of their lives waiting for something that will never happen!* We think we are justified in our resentment, but we waste a lot of energy nursing our grudge — *energy that could go towards building a better future.*

In reality, holding a grudge is often the first step on a path towards self-destruction. Prov. 14:30 says "A heart at peace gives life to the body, but envy rots the bones." Many studies of heart disease point to his fact[11]. That is why forgiveness is such a prominent theme in God's word. Unless we forgive others, we will

---

11   For example, see http://www.chce.research.va.gov/docs/pdfs/
pi_publications/Harris/2005_Harris_Thorsen_HF.pdf

never be as resilient, as optimistic or as in control of our lives as we could be.

The following is the sequence of freeing truths that God seeks to take each of us through when we need to become free of bitterness:

1. GOD'S CHARACTER IS FORGIVING

We need reminding that God is by nature forgiving, merciful and compassionate:

> *"For you, O Lord, are good and forgiving,*
> *abounding in steadfast love to all who call upon you.*
> *(Ps. 86:5)*

> *The LORD is merciful and gracious,*
> *slow to anger and abounding in steadfast love.*
> *He will not always chide,*
> *nor will he keep his anger forever.*
> *He does not deal with us according to our sins,*
> *nor repay us according to our iniquities.*
> *For as high as the heavens are above the earth,*
> *so great is his steadfast love toward those who fear him;*
> *as far as the east is from the west,*
> *so far does he remove our transgressions from us."*
> *(Psalm 103:8-12)*

2. GOD IN CHRIST FORGIVES US

Jesus has delivered us from the shame and the guilt of innumerable sins of thought, word, deed and omission. He has brought us into a glorious inheritance that we did not deserve:

> *"That is, in Christ God was reconciling the world*
> *to himself, not counting their trespasses against them,*

and entrusting to us the message of reconciliation." (2 Corinthians 5:19)

"In him we have redemption through his blood, the forgiveness of our trespasses, according to the riches of his grace." (Ephesians 1:7)

"He has delivered us from the domain of darkness and transferred us to the kingdom of his beloved Son, in whom we have redemption, the forgiveness of sins." (Colossians 1:13-14)

3. GOD CALLS US TO FORGIVE OTHERS

Our greatest motivation in forgiving others is to pass on freely to others what God has freely given to us:

"Let all bitterness and wrath and anger and clamor and slander be put away from you, along with all malice. Be kind to one another, tenderhearted, forgiving one another, as God in Christ forgave you." (Ephesians 4:31-32)

"For if you forgive others their trespasses, your heavenly Father will also forgive you." (Matthew 6:14)

"Then Peter came up and said to him, "Lord, how often will my brother sin against me, and I forgive him? As many as seven times?" Jesus said to him, "I do not say to you seven times, but seventy-seven times." (Matthew 18:21-22)

BECOMING FREE OF THE SINS OF OTHERS

A "root of bitterness" will have damaging effects in your life!

Strive for peace with everyone, and for the holiness without which no one will see the Lord. See to it that no one fails to

*obtain the grace of God; that no "root of bitterness" springs
up and causes trouble, and by it many become defiled.
(Hebrews 12:14-15)*

Jesus wants you to be free of grudges and their debilitating
effects, including medical problems, relational tensions, exces-
sive stress and worry, and the inability to move on and give your
attention to new ventures. Here are some ways that He wants to
empower you:

First, *we need to make a choice to forgive.* Living at peace with
others takes effort! Forgiveness does not come easily and it rarely
happens instantly. It may be helpful for you to think of forgiveness
as *a process — a series of choices that you make in order that you may be
free.* It may mean having to forgive the same person seventy-seven
times. You will need to choose to release anger that you have held
against the other person. You will need to choose to not stay in
a perpetual state of blaming them. However, over time and after
making many right choices, our heart will eventually follow what
we chose to do with our mind, mouth and actions.

Secondly, *I cannot stress enough the power that there is in praying
for and blessing those who offend you.* It is impossible to stay bitter
towards someone when you are asking God to bless them, even
when they have wounded you deeply. Lately, when I begin to
pray blessings into the lives of those who have hurt me I immediately feel my heart soften towards them. The good-will that I
feel in those moments is much better for my soul than ill-will that
makes me simply miserable. I dare you to try this right now! Jesus
instructs us to do this so that we will be free of the corrosive effect
of maintaining animosity in our hearts:

*Bless those who curse you, pray for those who abuse you.
(Luke 6:28)*

Thirdly, *we need to release people.* I have found that whenever
feelings of bitterness and victimization arise within me it helps me

to verbalize that that person(s) *owes me nothing.* If I continue to feel that they owe me something I remain stuck. I am trapped in a sense of entitlement that will only end *if* the other party apologizes and makes amends. *The entire matter and all of the outcomes must be released to God.* When I get to that point I feel truly free of the past and able to move on.

This is good news. Not only does Jesus deliver us from the power of our own sins, *He also delivers us from the entrapment of the sins of others!* When you follow the process that God has provided, you become increasingly free of the baggage from the past that you have been carrying. As you become free, you can anticipate a dramatic increase in your levels of peace, joy and contentment. You will have a newfound energy to be able to direct into building a brighter future. The injection of hope that you receive will improve your outlook and your prospects for a peace-filled life.

SETTING OTHERS FREE

A little known fact is that when God originally gave 'the Great Commandment' for his people to live by, he was speaking in the context of conflict resolution, dealing with grudges and choosing to not seek revenge:

> *"You shall not hate your brother in your heart, but you shall reason frankly with your neighbour, lest you incur sin because of him. You shall not take vengeance or bear a grudge against the sons of your own people, but you shall love your neighbour as yourself: I am the LORD". (Ex. 19:17-18)*

In other words, God is saying that you yourself know the heaviness that comes when someone else harbours bitterness of heart against you. *The best way to express love as the people of God is to not subject others to the heaviness of your unforgiveness.* To love your neighbour as yourself is to release them from their debt and release yourself from the effects of holding on to venomous spite. Release your debtors today!

FORGIVING YOUR SON'S KILLER

CBN.com reports an incredible story[12] that demonstrates both the difficulty of arriving at forgiveness and the great liberty that comes when you do forgive your debtor:

> *"That was it. Laramiun was gone," Mary Johnson said. "I'll never see him graduate, I'll never see him married, or see him have children. It seems unnatural for a parent to have to bury her child."*
>
> *On February 12th, 1993 Mary Johnson's only son Laramiun was killed by four gunshots, during a gang related altercation. With the help of eye witnesses, detectives found a prime suspect two days later.*
>
> *"I think hatred began to set in right then," Mary said.*
>
> *During a police investigation, 16 year old Oshea Israel confessed to killing Laramiun. After two years of hearings and appeals, he was tried as an adult and convicted of 2nd degree murder. Mary addressed him during her impact statement in court.*
>
> *"I said, 'You know what, if my son had taken your life, I would expect him to have to pay the cost,'... "And then I ended up telling him that I forgave him. The Word says in order to be forgiven, you must forgive. So I said, 'Okay, I have to tell him.' But I wanted him locked up, caged, because he was an animal and that is what he deserved."*

---

12   https://www.cbn.com/700club/features/amazing/ASH19_Mary_Johnson.aspx

Oshea was sentenced to 25 years in prison.

"The grieving process… began for me, after the trial," Mary said. "Wave after wave after wave — the tsunami — of just 'stuff.' Hatred. Here I am a Christian woman and I hated this 16 year old boy. And I never ever thought I would be put back together."

After the trial, Mary went through the motions of life. She visited friends and stayed active in her church. But it would be ten long years before her emotional turmoil would end. In 2004, her pastor asked her to teach a class on forgiveness. As the class studied the book, Mary says she took a hard look at her heart.

"I'm hearing, 'Mary, you need to repent. You need to repent for all these things that you've said about this young man. All these feelings that you've had for him,' And, I'm like [puffs] 'I have a right to have these feelings.'"

"Then I heard, 'Mary, pray for him like you pray for yourself.'…So I prayed for him like I pray for myself. Then I heard, 'Every time his name comes up, every time you hear it within yourself, say, 'I choose to forgive.' So, I repented and I really believe it was a true repentance. It was for real. "

As Mary started to change, so did the person she was praying for.

In 2005, Mary took another courageous step toward healing. She contacted the department of corrections and requested a face to face meeting with Oshea.

"I have to make sure I have truly forgiven him, that I don't have all that hatred," Mary said.

"I said 'Look, I told you in court that I forgave you. But today, from the bottom of my heart I want you to know that I forgive you,' Mary said. "And he was like, 'Ma'am how can you do that?' I said, 'Because of Who is in me.'"

"I felt like it was a very powerful and moving meeting," Oshea said. "I felt extremely compelled to ask her, 'May I give you a hug?' to show her my genuineness."

Mary said, "I do remember falling, and he had to hold me. He had to hold me up, until I felt this 'thing' leave me. And I instantly knew that all that hatred, the bitterness, the animosity, all that junk I had inside me for 12 years, I knew it was over with. It was done. Instantly, it was gone."

Mary and Oshea continued to meet and they eventually began speaking in prisons about forgiveness and reconciliation.

Oshea was released from prison in 2010, and Mary arranged his homecoming party. "I walked in and saw all of these people that I didn't know, who only knew of me because of the pain and the hurt I caused. But I walk in and get hugs. I walk in and get smiles," Oshea said. "That is another part of the forgiveness — the community forgave me, her friends were able to forgive me."

"I am so grateful for who I am today in God, that I am not that person that I used to be, full of all that junk," Mary said.

"Unforgiveness is a dangerous thing and I tell you when you allow the Holy Spirit to release you…oh my! What freedom! What freedom there is!" Mary said. "You'll be amazed at where you'll be in your life."

Isn't it amazing how Mary and Oshea, the forgiver and the forgiven, were both renewed, restored, and re-energized as all bitterness was laid down. God wants us all to be free in the same way.

This story also illustrates a counter-intuitive element in the process of healing- Mary was helped by intentionally walking towards the awkwardness and anxiety. When she moved towards the fear, she found out that nothing dreadful happened. Healing is often accelerated by exposure, but it is delayed by avoidance.

Not only do we need to forgive others, we may also need to forgive ourselves. If you put yourself in a position where you were vulnerable to getting hurt, or even if you *think* you may have, you may have a desire to punish yourself. Stop beating yourself up over mistakes made in the past. Allow yourself to make mistakes and take risks in life. How freeing it is to say, "I made a mistake. Human beings make mistakes. God forgives me and I forgive myself!" Allow his forgiveness over you to be *enough*, just as He says it is.

QUESTIONS FOR REFLECTION AND DISCUSSION:

1. Is there anyone in your life right now that you have been holding unforgiveness towards? Can you covenant in your heart to pray for that person and release them?

2. What benefits come into your life as you learn to forgive and release people?

3. Are there past mistakes in your own life that you haven't been able to forgive yourself for?

CHAPTER SEVEN:
CHOOSING YOUR FRIENDS =
CHOOSING YOUR FUTURE

Walk with the wise and become wise, for a companion of fools suffers harm.
(Prov. 13:20)

One of the most important things you can do in life is to *take the time to reflect deeply on where your relational choices and habits are taking you.* Friends will either add to or drain your emotional tank. The relational environments you place yourself in will largely determine your levels of satisfaction in life. Need proof?

Take a moment and chart out the years of your life to date. Simply draw a horizontal line across the bottom from left to right and divide it into years and decades. Then on the left side of the chart draw a vertical line to represent your level of enjoyment, happiness and satisfaction— write numbers ranging from one (at the bottom) up to ten (at the top). Now, starting from your childhood, draw a line that indicates the peaks and valleys of your enjoyment of life over the years. Then, draw a second dotted line that indicates the peaks and valleys of your relational life.

It is very likely that the peaks on your enjoyment of life line will align with those times when you were surrounded by loving and supportive friends! Likewise, the valleys will indicate times when you felt more isolated and unsupported. Amazing isn't it! Now my question to you is this: what are you doing now to influence the direction of that line in the future? Are you paying attention to who is in your inner circle? Are you putting time and effort into building positive support networks? Are you positioning yourself to work with people who are good for you?

When I chart my own life it is obvious that my levels of delight and contentment are highest when I have surrounded myself with people that I enjoy. I feed off of people that are quick to laugh, full of faith and willing to have an encouraging two-way friendship. I think of the enjoyment of doing life with my wife and the rich times we have enjoyed doing ministry together all over the world. I think of times when mentors gave of their time to speak truth into me and ensured that I would have the confidence and skills I would need to fulfill my calling. I think of a fly-fishing trip and missions trips with quality friends.

Reflecting back on my life affirms necessity of getting *intentional* about the type of people I most closely associate with. I am on a mission to unearth all of the wisdom that the scripture offers in this regard — both for my own journey and for yours.

It comes as a surprise to many people that the Bible has a great deal to say about the dangers of hanging out with draining people and the benefits of gathering around you trustworthy, life-giving people. Within the pages of the word of God, you will discover that *good people are one of the greatest resources available to you for energizing your God-given mission!*

Following are some poignant examples of people who understood the value of surrounding themselves with good people:

MOSES

Moses had the presence of mind to include people with deep wisdom in his inner circle, such as his father-in-law Jethro. As a result, in a season when the demands of leadership were greater than he could handle, he received sound advice to surround himself with quality individuals that would help him carry the load. Jethro helped Moses to *become sustainable* and to *avoid wearing himself out* by teaching him to share the load of responsibility (Ex. 18:18).

Jethro also gave Moses the criteria for selecting helpful supporting leaders. Think of this as a 'safety filter' that would ensure he had safe people around him. In Exodus 18:21 he was to look for people who were *able* (and competent), who *feared God* (and respected authority), who were *trustworthy* (and could be counted on), and who *hated a bribe* (and could not be manipulated). Future problems would be avoided by making careful team selections at the onset.

DAVID

David knew *he needed tested and loyal friends around him to support him in his God-given mission.* David tested the authenticity of offers of allegiance and support rather than just taking promises of support at face value. As a result he had people around him that were legendary in their support (1 Chron. 12:17-18)! David also allowed into his inner circle the trustworthy Jonathan, Saul's son, who "*strengthened his hand in God*" when he needed support the most (1 Sam. 23:16).

Additionally, David placed people in his court that he could receive counsel from. He even had one man, Hushai the Archite, *who had the sole job of being the kings friend* (1 Chron. 27:33)! The king was essentially saying: "I am carrying a lot of responsibility. I need people around me who are devoted, reliable, perceptive and discerning. Your assignment, should you choose to accept it, is to stay in relational connection and proximity to me so that through friendship you can shore up my efforts. Since friendship is a mutual endeavour, I will also be a resource to you so I can help you fulfill your God-given assignment." So effective was this measure that David's son Solomon also made sure that he had a friend at his side, Zabud the Son of Nathan, to help him in the pressure cooker of his responsibilities (1 Kings 4:5)!

JEHOIADA

The priest Jehoiada knew that the young king Joash *would need good men around him if he was going to secure his throne in a hostile environment.* Jehoiada took courage and went on a campaign to secure the loyalty of the leaders throughout the nation — which they gave freely. He even instructed the Levites to "surround the king, each with his weapons in his hand" (2 Chron. 23:7). Because of the careful planning of Jehoiada, *the young king had dependable and honourable people around him that were committed to seeing him protected and flourishing.* Thus Joash was positioned for success and was able to restore the worship of the nation.

NEHEMIAH

Nehemiah knew he needed good people around him when he worked with great zeal to see the city of Jerusalem rebuilt as a thriving center for his people. In Ezra 8:16 he sent for nine leaders that were "*men of insight*" who helped him in turn to add to his team a man of "discretion". He also had on-board the prophets of God who supported the effort by declaring truth (Ezra 5:1). *In order to accomplish the task he had to have the best of associations around him.* Any great vision will be accomplished as a result of many capable and competent people surrounding you and contributing, whether you are building a family, a ministry or a nation.

PAUL

Paul knew that *he needed good people around him if he was going to complete his assignment of bringing the gospel to the nations.* In fact, he chose as his closest associate Barnabas, who was known at 'the encourager' by people who knew him well! There would be many people who would make life difficult for Paul, so he needed people close to him who would bring refreshing Such friendships would offset and surpass the effect of draining people. *Refreshing people were so important to* him that he often mentioned them by name in his letters and expressed deep appreciation for them (see 2 Tim. 1:16 and 2 Cor.7:6-7).

WALK WITH THE WISE

I can't emphasize enough the importance of getting around people that are good for you. My life is a case in point and so is yours! When I am around people who are negative, critical, petty or arrogant my emotional state tends to take a downward spiral. Conversely, when I am around people who are positive, full of faith, encouraging and kind, I feel that I can take on the world!

We pay attention to the kind of soil we plant a seed in, but we don't often enough consider the type of relational soil we are planting our dreams in. Are the people nearest you the best choices to help you pursue your highest goals and values in the short time you have been given? Sometimes one of the most healthy moves we can make is admitting to ourselves that we have to plant our dreams in better relational soil.

There is wide variety in the severity of negative circumstances and people around you. Often you will need to remove yourself from the source of stress for a short time. In other cases it needs to be a long term move. Do not allow your pride and your desire to 'tough out' a situation put you at risk of more permanent damage to your soul! *You should be more concerned about the condition of your soul than the discomfort of making a change in a relationship, a job or lifestyle.* At the very least you will need to teach people around you how to treat you if the same level of access to your life is going to continue.

To help you evaluate the benefit of relationships around you, I am giving you an indication of qualities I am looking for in comrades and partners at this stage in my life. I look for people who have handled adversity in their life well and are now better rather than bitter. I want to spend time with people who have a sense of humour and a positive outlook on life. I want to be around people who are safe in terms of understanding the effects of their words on others. I am inspired by people who are moving towards their 'sweet spot' in life rather than settling for second best. I need to spend quality time with people who prioritize God's will for their lives and are always dreaming new dreams.

There have been several seasons in my life when it was important for me to re-evaluate the effect that friends were having on me. The first was in high school when I came to faith in Christ. I had a lot of friends at the time that I enjoyed many activities with. The only problem was that when we spent time together we would always manage to end up in some type of trouble! I was tired of being influenced to do things that I would later regret. One night, when my friends and I were bored, we went out walking through the streets of our town where we ran into a drunk man. My friend thought it would be funny to try to talk to him, but it wasn't funny when he pulled a handgun on us! We made it to safety, but it was clear that I needed to shift more of my time to those who would influence me towards productive activities that would lead me towards a better future and the things of God. Amazingly, I found that the quality of my life tracked with the quality of friends I spent time with!

Another season that comes to mind is my college days. The young adult years are so critical because we are making so many direction-setting decisions that follow us for life. It was during this time that I became friends with a fun-loving guy named Gary that I had been on ministry trips with, including a three country tour in Africa. Later we served on faculty at the same college and had great times together as families. Now, many years later, this friendship has continued to be a life-line for me although we are separated by many miles. One of the most replenishing trips I have taken was a fly-in fishing trip with a group of friends at his family's cabin. Also, our entire family looks forward to those occasions when we can get together as a visit because we have so much fun and we provide mutual encouragement for one another. Whether it is a pep talk before heading into nerve-wracking contract negotiations or being able to decompress after difficult meetings, these friends have brought incredible refreshing. It is one of the greatest blessings in life to have friends who know you deeply, and yet are still your greatest cheerleaders!

The apostle Paul often spoke of friends like this, like Onesiphorus, who "often refreshed me" (2 Tim. 1:16) and Philemon, through whom the hearts of Christians had been "refreshed". We all need friends like this!

Finally, lest you get the sense that this business of friendship is easy, I want you to know that this has been a challenging area in my life. For one thing, I can be quite private and goal-driven, so I often need to push myself to make investments into friendships. At times I have also been too slow to move on from unhelpful people or situations. But perhaps the greatest challenge that I have faced is that the nature of my work has meant that we have moved fairly often. This means that extra effort is needed to establish new friendships, maintain older friendships and discern whether friendships need to be nurtured or put on passive mode. Yet, whatever the challenge, I am committed for the long-term to have a relationally satisfying life for myself and to be a supportive friend to others.

The following are some of the insights on friendship from C.S. Lewis that are informing and inspiring me at this stage in life, and

I trust that they will do the same for you (the first is from "The Collected Letters of C.S. Lewis, Volume 2" and the remainder are from "The Four Loves"):

> "Friendship is the greatest of all worldly goods.
> Certainly to me it is the chief happiness of life.
> If I had to give a piece of advice to a young man
> about a place to live, I think I should say, 'sacrifice
> almost everything to live where you can be near
> your friends.'"

> "There is no safe investment. To love at all is to be
> vulnerable. Love anything and your heart will be
> wrung and possibly broken. If you want to make
> sure of keeping it intact you must give it to no one,
> not even an animal. Wrap it carefully round with
> hobbies and little luxuries; avoid all entanglements.
> Lock it up safe in the casket or coffin of your selfish-
> ness. But in that casket, safe, dark, motionless, airless,
> it will change. It will not be broken; it will become
> unbreakable, impenetrable, irredeemable. To love is to
> be vulnerable."

> "Those who have nothing can share nothing; those
> who are going nowhere can have no fellow-travelers."

> "People who bore one another should meet seldom;
> people who interest one another, often."

> "Affection is responsible for nine-tenths of what-
> ever solid and durable happiness there is in our
> natural lives."

> "...as Friendship strengthens, it will do this even
> when my Friends are far away."

"In a perfect Friendship this Appreciative love is,
I think, often so great and so firmly based that
each member of the circle feels, in his secret heart,
humbled before the rest. Sometimes he wonders
what he is doing there among his betters. He is lucky
beyond desert to be in such company. Especially
when the whole group is together; each bringing
out all that is best, wisest, or funniest in all the others.
Those are the golden sessions; when four or five of us
after a hard day's walk have come to our inn; when
our slippers are on, our feet spread out toward the
blaze and our drinks are at our elbows; when the
whole world, and something beyond the world, opens
itself to our minds as we talk; and no one has any
claim on or any responsibility for another, but all are
freemen and equals as if we had first met an hour ago,
while at the same time an Affection mellowed by the
years enfolds us. Life — natural life — has no better
gift to give. Who could have deserved it?"

A TALE OF TWO PRINCES

Once upon a time, in a college far, far away there were two young princes (we called them students!). My wife and I loved pouring ourselves into these students, affirming them in their giftedness and giving them opportunities to spread their wings. From that place we were delighted to see students disperse all over the world and live lives of impact.

The first student was a great guy. Wherever he went you would find a circle of people around him cracking up because of his antics and zany sense of humour. He would have been the leading candidate for the 'most likely to be a stand-up comedian' award. He was full of potential and related well to people. Sadly, he did not think through the issue of how his friends would, to a large degree, influence his future. He chose friends that were irresponsible and lazy at best and frivolous and rebellious at worst.

Several years later we were on a road trip and popped into a Burger King to grab a quick bite to eat. A guy in the back was calling to another guy, saying, "Dude, what are you doing? Are you trying to hide from someone?" Then out from the back of the restaurant came our former student looking rather sheepish. Now, let me be clear that we like this guy and it is not that it is wrong to work at Burger King, but we both knew that the choices of friends he had made had led him down a path that was far below his potential.

The second student was also a great guy. He made wise choices in terms of his friends. We sometimes equate walking in wisdom with being prudish, but that was certainly not the case with this young man. He seemed to have a hand in all of the practical jokes on campus during his era! But all the while he was surrounding himself with people who knew how to have good clean fun, work hard, walk with God and be committed to friends and family. Today he is thriving in his family life, his business and his contribution to the community.

You may have heard that you will attain to the average income of your five closest friends! The reality is that we become like those we spend time with. Our friends and our environment shape us and the way we think. Are your five closest friends going where you want to go in terms of not only their finances, but also their marriages?

Their values? Their attitudes? Their legacy?

Show me your friends and I will show you your future!

QUESTIONS FOR REFLECTION AND DISCUSSION:

1. Do you have people in your life that provide comfort, joy and/or refreshing when you go through disconcerting seasons in life?

2. Are there friends or mentors in your life who help you stay on track?

3. How can you better position yourself to be in life-giving relationships?

4. What would you say are the Biblical marks of a good friend?

CHAPTER EIGHT:
PERMISSION TO REST

"Are you tired? Worn out? Burned out on religion? Come to me. Get away with me and you'll recover your life. I'll show you how to take a real rest. Walk with me and work with me—watch how I do it. Learn the unforced rhythms of grace. I won't lay anything heavy or ill-fitting on you. Keep company with me and you'll learn to live freely and lightly."
(Matthew 11:28-30, The Message)

One of my favourite all-time stories is the Lumberjack Story[13]:

It was the annual lumberjack competition and in the final was an older experienced lumberjack and a younger, stronger lumberjack. Whoever could fell the most trees in a day would be the winner.

The younger lumberjack was full of enthusiasm and went off into the woods and set to work straight away. As he worked he could hear the older lumberjack working in another part of the forest, and he felt more and more confident with every swift swing of his axe that he would win.

At regular intervals throughout the day the noise of trees being felled in the other part of the forest would stop. The

---

13   Popularized by Steven Covey in *7 Habits of Highly Effective People*, as quoted in: http://juvenate-ltd.com/lumberjack-story/effort

younger lumberjack took heart from this reasoning that the old man was tiring out, whereas he could use his superior youth and strength to keep going.

At the end of the competition the younger lumberjack felt tired but confident he had won as he scanned the piles of felled trees that were the result of his superhuman effort.

At the medal ceremony he stood on the podium expecting to be awarded the prize of champion lumberjack. Next to him stood the older lumberjack who looked surprisingly less exhausted than he felt.

When the results were read out he was devastated to hear that the older lumberjack had chopped down significantly more trees than he had. He turned to the older lumber jack and said, "How can this be? I heard you take a rest every hour and I worked continuously. I am stronger and fitter than you old man".

The older lumberjack turned to him and said, "Every hour I took a break to rest and sharpen my saw."

The point is that, contrary to what our culture believes, *you will be more effective in every part of your life if you take time to sharpen your saw*! This means taking adequate time for personal rest and refuelling — and it is more important now than ever before.

Most adults today are just plain tired, overworked and overwhelmed. Even younger people are often choosing to keep a harried schedule or are pressured into doing so by driven parents. The more our lives speed up, the more likely we are to feel exhausted and frayed. Rarely does our existence feel light. Our typical greeting becomes, "I am so busy". It is both a badge of honour and an admittance that our lives are out of control!

Let's do a little survey to see how many limitations on your time you're running up against. You can assess your level of busyness and your need for rest by thinking through your answers to these clarifying questions. *Are you feeling fully rested and relaxed or are you absolutely exhausted? If something does not go according to plan or schedule are you OK or do you feel it puts you at a breaking point? Are you getting adequate sleep or do you regularly complain of not having had a long enough sleep?*

- *Are your energy reserves such that you can respond to opportunities that come up or are you 'maxed-out'?*

- *Are your loved ones getting some of your prime time and attention, or your left-overs?*

- *Are you operating at a pace that you can maintain or are you always operating at your peak output levels (with the constant gnawing feeling that something is about to snap)?*

- *Are you putting energy into people and initiatives that are high values for you or is it drained away by secondary concerns?*

How did you do? *If your answers are balanced towards the former scenario in each question then you are well on your way to living a sustainable lifestyle.* You are in alignment with the reality of your need to steward your limited time and energies well. *If your answers are balanced towards the later scenarios then you are living your life according to myths.* You think that you can live without rest, that the important people in your life will wait indefinitely for your attention and that you will always have *tomorrow.* You need a reality check!

CREATING MARGIN

If you need permission to rest you are in the majority in our society. Dr. Richard Swenson, in his book "*Margin*" says that we are a piled-on, stretched-to-the-limit society where a lot of people are headed for a crash. People are sleeping less hours and working more hours than their grandparent's generation did. Our frantic, technology-driven lifestyles leave us with lower reserves of time and energy in our lives. We are exponentially busy and rarely 'unplugged'. To help combat this trend, Swenson gives *four benefits of building margin into your life*[14]:

Peace of mind. When you're not hurrying and worrying all the time, you have time to think. Time to relax. Time to enjoy life. Time to enjoy beauty. Time to worship. Time to regain your composure and cultivate a restful spirit.

Better health. Unrelenting stress harms our bodies. We all know that, yet we let it continue day after day after day. Why do we wait until our health plummets before we make this decision? Why not realize that we need to build some margin into our lives *now*? The truth is, your body needs downtime in order to heal. Race cars make pit stops occasionally in order to get repaired, refuelled and maintained. You can't fix anything going 200 miles an hour! Yet we try to be repaired and refuelled while we're still racing through life. Margin builds in time for better health.

Stronger relationships. Lack of margin is one big reason for the collapse of the family today. When we don't make relationships a priority and make time for each other, our relationships suffer. The truth is, relationships take time, and margin provides the time to sit and talk, to listen to and enjoy one another and to provide the company we all need.

Usefulness in ministry. When you're overloaded by activity, you can only think of yourself. You are in survival mode, just trying to make it through another day. But being available to God for his purposes makes all the difference in this world. When you have no margin in your life, and God taps you on the shoulder and says, "I'd like you to do this for me," your first response isn't joy. Your first response is, "Oh, no! Another thing to do! Sorry, God. I'd like to do that, but I'm just too busy." *But when you have margin, you're available to God.* I'm not talking about you being available for how

---

14   *Margin*, by Richard A. Swenson (Colorado Springs: NavPress, 1992).

other people think you should be used — very often those are the very activities we need to weed out of our lives to create margin! You know, the ones imposed on us by others that we didn't have the heart to say no to. I'm talking about being available for the real God-given opportunities that suit your giftings and callings.

Have you ever stopped to calculate what *not* taking adequate rest and *not* recharging your batteries may be costing you? The costs may include:

Being too exhausted to put energy into friendships.
Feeling your entire life is consumed by obligation.
Forgetting how to play and how to savour life.
Losing your passion for the things you care most about.
Looking for escape instead of restoration.
Impairing your ability to make good decisions.
Being unable to contribute to worthy projects with gusto.
Having no energy for your family.
Compromising your health/physical capacity.

SHORTER SHIFTS

As I write this chapter the winter Olympics are being televised and the most watched sport in Canada is men's hockey. One of the most common topics mentioned by commentators is 'shift time'. Team Canada's coach has shortened the time he expects players to be on the ice from 50 seconds to a mere 40 seconds per shift. This means that at all times Team Canada has 'fresh legs' on the ice and they rarely, if ever, have a defensive breakdown. It is no wonder that with this strategy they have showed dominance and earned another gold medal.

Contrast this to some of the guys I have played recreational hockey with! Inevitably there will be a guy on the ice that is still surprised that he was never drafted into the NHL! He wanders around on the ice for three minutes while better and more rested players sit on the bench. If you have a player like this on your team it is very hard to win. Don't be that guy! Think of the impact your 'long shifts' are having on those closest to you.

The good news is that you don't have to live on overload. You don't have to live in survival mode. You can learn to pace yourself. In fact, God himself invites and gives you *permission to rest*! God in his infinite goodness understands the way that we are made and provides for us one of the greatest means available to human beings for refreshing — the Sabbath. In his infinite goodness He says, "You cannot be running at full tilt all the time and still enjoy life as I meant you to live — take one seventh of the time off to renew yourself physically, emotionally and spiritually"!

In His wisdom, God gives you permission to catch your breath, but unfortunately, the pace of most people's lives in the West is too fast to utilize the restorative power of rest. The following truths bring sanity, balance and correction to the pacing of our lives:

Rest begins with an attitude of trust. "It is in vain that you rise up early and go late to rest, eating the bread of anxious toil; for He gives to his beloved sleep" (Psalm 127:2). God wants to give you rest today. He wants you to live a life that's focused on Him. He wants you to experience a life of peace, joy and attentiveness to His activity in our lives. *Our drivenness in ministry and in our businesses often comes from an unhealthy place — we think that it all depends on us. Not so!* We need to do our part and diligently apply ourselves, but all the while we need to take pauses. Through this we can cultivate a serenity of heart based on the confidence that *God can do more in a moment than we can accomplish in a lifetime!*

As I have seen demands on my schedule increase I have been learning to pray something like this, "Lord, we have done all that we can with the time we have available. We are making our best effort to be strategic and to follow Your leading and wisdom. We are taking a rest now so that we will be sustainable for the long haul. While we take our breather, we ask that You would bring to us the favour, bookings and connections that we need in the coming months? Thank You that in your kindness You allow us space to rest

— I receive it as a gift". As we have done that I have been encouraged that many of the 'seeds' that we planted in our time of activity resulted in a 'harvest' in our time of rest. Learn to do less and to trust God more.

Rest is meant to be for our refreshing. "Six days you shall do your work, but on the seventh day you shall rest; that… the son of your servant woman, and the alien, may be refreshed" (Ex. 23:12). The Biblical instruction on Sabbath rest for God's people focuses on the purpose of the rest rather than describing exactly how that should look. There is room within the call to rest to do what we find personally restorative. That may include quiet time, time to enjoy the outdoors, time to read or time with family. Sadly, much of our 'recreation' today leaves us *more* exhausted than our regular routines! Our most recent holiday, which was our first real "vacation", had its awesome moments, but often felt like a marathon of running away from loud partiers at the resort!

Rest is meant to be relational and worshipful. The original intention of the Sabbath was that there would be a God-ward component as the people of God were to gather for re-orienting their lives around Him. "The seventh day is a Sabbath of solemn rest, a holy convocation" (Ex. 23:3). Their rest was to be a weekly reminder that they were a people that had been set apart *by* and *for* the Lord.

As I write this chapter I am listening to Bethel Worship and Kim Walker of Jesus Culture Music on YouTube. Worship lifts us up from whatever is depleting us. Focusing on God, his character and His ability, replenishes and calms the soul. Being in a state of praise and adoration puts you in a frame of mind where you remember what matters in life. It is good for my soul to take pause in the process of writing and raise my arms to God in recognition of the steadfast love that He has shown me.

Rest is meant to be part of a sustainable rhythm of living. As a loving Father, God modelled rest for us! "For in six days the Lord made heaven and earth, the sea, and all that is in them, and rested on the seventh day. Therefore the Lord blessed the Sabbath day and made it holy" (Exodus 20:11). Now, God did not require the rest because He is infinite in power, but he took this break for instructional purposes. As our Creator, He knows that we *need* space for feasting, playing, and fellowshipping. *Rest for our souls is as essential to our health as air is for breathing and food is for eating.*

Rest is meant to be a reprieve from a life of endless toil. "Better is a handful of quietness than two hands full of toil and a striving after wind. Again, I saw vanity under the sun: one person who has no other, either son or brother, yet there is no end to all his toil, and his eyes are never satisfied with riches, so that he never asks, 'For whom am I toiling and depriving myself of pleasure?' This also is vanity and an unhappy business" (Ecclesiastes 4:6-8). There is great potential to derive enjoyment from work that you love, but to toil endlessly for riches is to live a one-dimensional life that is "an unhappy business" indeed!

Rest is meant to be a reminder that we are free. "You shall remember that you were a slave in the land of Egypt, and the Lord your God brought you out from there with a mighty hand and an outstretched arm. Therefore the LORD your God commanded you to keep the Sabbath day" (Deuteronomy 5:15). Mark Buchanan wrote an excellent book on this subject entitled *The Rest of God: Restoring Your Soul by Restoring Sabbath.* In it he reminds us that the same God who created us wants us to live a liberated existence. He wants us to remember that we are slaves to no one. Our rest is a reminder to ourselves and to the world that we are subject to no one but God.

LEAVE THE GOVERNANCE OF THE UNIVERSE TO GOD

The cold hard reality is that we are either situating ourselves for burn-out by not having a regular pattern of rest, or we are situating ourselves for replenishment by enjoying a Sabbath lifestyle. For me, enjoying the Sabbath often includes getting a good night's sleep (read: I am going to sleep in!), taking a more leisurely approach to my quiet time with God, exercising and spending some quality time with my family. I also enjoy spending time reading a good book and perhaps getting together with friends. At the same time, I am learning to resist the temptation to make that a day to get caught up on home renovation projects because that leaves me *less* invigorated for the week ahead. I am learning to focus on activities that are therapeutic (i.e. they do not feel like work!). As I do this, I am finding that the greatest value in observing the Sabbath is that it reboots my perspective on life as my 'encouragement bucket' is filled.

Finally, I want to emphasize that God is as much concerned about the disposition of our hearts as the observation of a day of rest. He wants you to learn to have a stillness of heart and an orientation of trust. He wants to transform the way you see yourself and the way you see your place in the world. He wants you to recognize His place as Creator and your place as creature. He wants you to rest without guilt. He wants you to carry the conviction that He is both good and sovereign — so you can *relax*.

This story illustrates the point well:

> *Philip Melanchthon and Martin Luther were once deciding on the day's agenda. The former was disciplined, intellectually gifted, serious, and goal-driven; the latter was equally intelligent but much more emotional, risky, even playful.*
>
> *Melanchthon said, "Martin, this day we will discuss the governance of the universe."*
>
> *To which Luther responded, "Philip, this day you and I will go fishing and leave governance of the universe to God."*[15]

Think of all that you have to gain from adopting a more restful mindset and lifestyle!

---

15   http://daily.insight.org/site/News2?page=NewsArticle&id=7551

QUESTIONS FOR REFLECTION AND DISCUSSION:

1. Does your life feel like constant motion? Take a good hard look at your personal, family and work schedule.

2. Is this a pace that you and your family can sustain without running on empty or without important values being neglected?

3. Are you in the habit of taking some time each week to be restored and refreshed spiritually, or is this something that is sorely lacking from your life?

4. What changes can I make in the next 48 hours?

CHAPTER NINE:
NOURISHING YOUR SPIRITUAL LIFE

Have you not known? Have you not heard? The Lord is the everlasting God, the Creator of the ends of the earth. He does not faint or grow weary; his understanding is unsearchable. He gives power to the faint, and to him who has no might he increases strength. Even youths shall faint and be weary, and young men shall fall exhausted; but they who wait for the Lord shall renew their strength; they shall mount up with wings like eagles; they shall run and not be weary; they shall walk and not faint. (Is. 40:28-31)

Are you feeling replenished and healthy spiritually? Progress in every other area of life will leave you all the more empty if you do not acknowledge that in the very nature of how you were created you have spiritual needs. Your spirit is at the core of your being. It is your God-given capacity to relate to your Creator. The Bible says that God "put eternity into man's heart" (Eccl. 3:11). We put a lot of thought into other areas of our lives, but how much thought do you put into being in right relationship with your Creator?

I grew up in a very religious family — my parents religiously drank Pilsner beer! I first heard the gospel as a child when invited by friends to a backyard vacation Bible school club and then later at a Boys Club at a local church that taught boys woodworking and the Scriptures. I was delighted to discover that although I was a sinner, Christ still loved me and demonstrated his love for me by dying on the cross for my sins. I still remember the surge of love and appreciation that gushed up from my heart when I heard the news. It was then that I opened my heart to the love of Christ.

If you have never entered into a personal relationship with Jesus Christ I urge you to do so today. If you are exploring what this means, then the best resource is, of course, reading the Bible, but I also recommend: (1) taking a local Alpha course so that you can explore Christianity in a safe environment (*alpha.org*), (2) reading Lee Strobel's *The Case for Faith* to help you with difficult questions you may have and (3) exploring *powertochange.org* to find out more about what it means to know Jesus personally.

Choosing to follow Jesus Christ today takes a lot of courage, but it is more than worth it! I once had the opportunity to take a team to share the gospel in some of the largest prisons in the Baltic nation of Estonia. We were greeted by razor wire and Soviet era surroundings that were so grim that they reminded me of WWII concentration camps. It was one of the most dangerous and potentially volatile environments I have ever been in.

However, when we shared about the hope we had found in Christ, about a dozen men boldly indicated that they also wanted to follow Christ! Immediately I thought about what may happen to them for publicly professing Christ *in prison!* But they took the words of Christ that we spoke seriously: "*So everyone who acknowledges me before men, I also will acknowledge before my Father who is in heaven, but whoever denies me before men, I also will deny before my Father who is in heaven*" (Mt. 10:32-33). I knew that their great courage would one day be rewarded. If you haven't yet done so, make the same bold step today.

Although I first placed my faith in Christ as a child, it was not until I was fifteen years old that I discovered more of what it meant to have a living, vibrant relationship with God. I was taken under the wings of the aunt and uncle of a good friend of mine. They showed me that committing my life to Christ was only the first step of a journey that would last a lifetime and stretch into eternity. This family was not wealthy by human standards, but they enriched my understanding by allowing me to get close enough to see what following Christ meant in the details of life.

If they didn't have enough money to pay the bills they would sit down at the kitchen table and pray *"Lord, we know that you are God our provider. We believe that we are here in this town on an assignment from you. We pray that you'd step in and take care of this. Amen."* When they found what kind of posters I had on the wall in my room and what kind of music I listened to, they patiently explained to me what a life that pleased God looked like. When they found out I was involved in occult-related activities, they explained to me that there was real demonic power to break from and they led my friends and I in prayer as we built a bonfire with the occult materials. Mostly, however, they modelled what walking with God was like, and that held great attraction for me. It was through their influence, and the influence of others, that I began to take my first uncertain steps as a Christ follower.

As I took these steps and was baptized I noticed that not everyone around me shared my new enthusiasm. I was shocked to see people that had grown up in Christian homes abandoning all that they ever knew of the things of God. I was naïve and I was heartbroken. It was then that church-going folks introduced a new word into my vocabulary — 'backsliding'.

Clearly a vibrant spiritual life was not something that came automatically — it had to be *nurtured* and *protected*. In those early years of following Christ I learned something that became more and more unmistakable — *that every day of our lives we make choices that leave us spiritually depleted or renewed.* The attitudes we adopt, the disciplines we commit to and the relationships we prioritize all affect the vibrancy of our relationship with God. We either position ourselves for spiritual freshness or dryness.

One of the ways that Jesus described this positioning was *by comparing the orientation of your heart to the condition of soil.* In Luke 8 he spoke of four inclinations of the heart as being like these four types of soil: (1) *hardened,* (2) *shallow,* (3) *choked out* or (4) *fertile.*

The seed that is thrown on the soil represents the word of God. The word of God is our primary means of spiritual nourishment and growth. It has the power of life and multiplication within it. Inherent within it is the potential to multiply into thirty, sixty or a hundred times what was sown. *It is guaranteed to produce fruit if and when it falls on rich, well-watered, fertile soil.*

WHAT IS THE CONDITION OF YOUR HEART?

The first soil is *hardened* and rocky so the word of God bounces off of it and is unable to release the power of life and multiplication within it. This represents a heart that has become hardened to the working of God — it will never receive the life-giving benefits available to it.

The second soil is *shallow*. It represents a heart that initially is attracted to the things of God but it does not allow the seed to put roots down deep. It is a heart that also misses out on the life-giving blessings available to it.

The third soil is *choked out*. It is infested by the weeds of life's worries, riches and pleasures. It represents a heart that is so cluttered that the life of God has no space within it to flourish.

The fourth soil, Jesus explains, is *cultivated, deep, and free of weeds*. It is *fertile* and ready to receive. This final soil represents those who have a good and noble heart, who hear the word, retain it and produce a crop by persevering. The most important thing you bring into your spiritual life and your relationship with God is a heart that makes space for the word of God to flourish. It is not a cluttered heart. It is a heart that is committed to protecting the work of God within it.

What I want you to notice is that the crop that should be expected in each of these scenarios is entirely knowable and *predictable*. If the predisposition of the heart is hardness or shallowness or distractedness, we expect virtually no crop! But if the heart is predisposed towards receiving the Word and allowing it to do its work *over a long period of time* — then we can know with certainty that the multiplying life of the Word in our lives will indeed take effect. Fruit *will* happen, both in us and through us!

WAYS TO RENEW YOUR SPIRITUAL LIFE

Now we turn our attention to some of the practical ways that we can take responsibility for nurturing our spiritual lives and renewing our love for God. We are all well aware of how we need to grow in our relationship with Him. My priority here is not to reproduce abundant material that has already been written about spiritual practices or 'means of grace' available to the Christ follower, but rather to share with you a short-list of ways that I am getting traction and living a spiritually renewed life:

1. Keeping A Thankfulness Journal

In her book "*Who Shut Off My Brain*", Dr. Carolyn Leaf tells us that studies in neuroscience confirm what we already knew in Christian theology — that your level of thankfulness truly forms who you become as a person. When a person has negative thoughts (such as self-pity or helplessness) or if they interpret an event negatively (such as thinking that the actions of someone else diminished them as a person), then chemicals produced actually attempt to find other similar thoughts and feelings. Dr. Leaf explains that this is like vines or branches finding each other and becoming intertwined and reinforced. This is how, over time, people develop a jaded, embittered and otherwise cranky view of life!

The good news is that the opposite effect can be generated! When a person cultivates a healthy thought life and interprets events through the lens of the goodness of God and His capability to work all things for our good, then the chemicals produced link up with other like thoughts and reinforce them. The entire process is called neuroplasticity. You can intentionally nurture emotional health, personal renewal and spiritual resiliency through this process! You can literally renew your mind!

The way I cultivate this in my life is by journaling all the things for which I can be grateful to God. I call this my "thankfulness journal". Typically, during my daily quiet time with the LORD, I take the time to list everything I can think of in my life for which to express gratitude to God. The Bible is clear that everything good in our lives — every bit of blessing, benefit and bounty — is a personal gift from God that communicates his unchanging and generous nature (James 1:17). Though my emotions or my circumstances may try to tell me otherwise, there on the page in front of me is evidence that God is for me and I have much to be encouraged about. I am reminded that at the proper time there will be a harvest if I do not give up (Gal. 6:9).

Thankfulness journaling helps you get rid of fatalism and a sense of futility that robs you of hope and energy. On some days your list of blessings will flow and on other days you will need to more strongly discipline your thinking (often I will challenge myself to reach a certain number, like 30 or 50 things I am thankful for). *By focusing on things that are going right in your life you are energized for the day*!

2. Being Mentored By the Holy Spirit

I had the opportunity to do my 'devotions' with a spiritual hero of mine, Wayne Cordiero, and a group of leaders in Vancouver. We were all eager to learn how to be more consistent in seeking God and how to place ourselves where we could regularly hear from God. Wayne introduced us to a method of being mentored by the Holy Spirit through Scripture reading and journaling. He introduced us to the best reading guide I have found to date that takes you through the Old Testament once and the New Testament twice in a year. You can find the guide at *lifejournal.cc*. Whether you follow this pattern or another one, you need to eat daily of the Word of God so that you do not become spiritually malnourished.

It never ceases to amaze me how there will be something from a daily Bible reading that will nourish me in what I am going through in the current season of my life. Equally important is the fact that over time you are building *a reservoir of wisdom* that you can draw on when you face life's challenges.

3. Being With Genuine Christ-followers

I have already elaborated on the vital importance that associations play in our lives. Your connection to (or lack of connection to) passionate Christ followers is as much a factor in your devotion to Christ as any other factor. I see this all the time. People who do not make the effort to fellowship are shocked and perplexed to find that their devotion to Christ wanes and they then cannot overcome problems on their own. On the other hand, those who go out of their way to associate with good-hearted, kingdom-minded people enjoy the benefits of mutual encouragement and inspiration.

4. Reading Material That Supports Your Faith

Are you exposing yourself to content that inspires you, equips you and informs you? Experience has shown me that I am far more motivated when I build motivation into my routine through daily inspirational reading! It helps me to not plateau and keeps me in a mindset of learning and growth. I thank God almost daily for the proven insights I have found that have saved me from vocational stagnation, unsafe people, financial slavery and spiritual lethargy. For a list of the top books that have been life-changing for me personally go to "Resource Three — Recommended Reading" in the appendix. A note of caution here... be careful that everything you read is carefully filtered through the truth God's word.

5. Varying Your Approach

One of the common mistakes people make that keeps them in a state of spiritual inertia is that they do not vary their approach.

Always be on the lookout for ways that you can position yourself sto experience the grace that God has provided to you. Be creative and discover how you may open yourself up to God's presence with you. For example:

- Take a walk and enjoy the beauty and grandeur of the created world

- Watch an uplifting worship video on youtube

- Read prayers from the Psalms or from a book of prayer

- Write out your prayers

- Offload your concerns to God in prayer

- Bring someone else's needs to God in prayer

- Spend time quietly thinking about the character and attributes of God

- Listen in silence for what God wants to say to you

- Repeat a phrase or verse from scripture in order to focus your attention and to help you rest in God's presence

- Imagine Christ present with you, or visualize God on His throne in heaven as the apostle John describes Him in Revelation

- Ask God which creative ideas He may want you to pursue in your work life

- Confess attitudes, actions, or thoughts which are hindering your relationship with God

- Practice the presence of God during the day by frequently turning your thoughts to Him

- Start your day in a peaceful manner by having a quiet time with God rather than rushing

- Change your posture in prayer — kneeling, lying prostrate, lifting arms or walking

- Use different types of fasting (voluntary denial of an other-wise normal function, such as eating, watching TV, sweets, etc.) for the sake of spiritual focus and prayer

- Listen to the the Bible on audio and uplifting podcasts as you drive, work, or rest

- Use online resources or your Bible computer software to prayerfully interact with scripture

- Sit on your deck-swing with a good cup of coffee and just enjoy being with God

- If you play an instrument or like to sing, spend some time singing or playing to the Lord in worship

- If you are an artist, spend time expressing worship to Him through your art

6. Soaking in the Presence of God

I love reading about how characters in the Bible were developed into instruments that God could use. In Exodus 33:7-11 we read about how the young Joshua, the aid to Moses, would linger in the presence of God, long after Moses had left. Those extended times of soaking in God's presence had a profound effect on who Joshua became.

In these times he learned *to define himself in terms of who God was, rather than by what unbelieving people around him thought.* When he was sent on the mission to spy out the land promised to them by God, he saw other young leaders around him abdicating the abundance that God had for His people. They were shaped by the size of the problem, but he was shaped by the majesty of God. He did not want to become like them! At all costs he would not be defined by negativity, doubt and self-pity. He trained himself to not focus on the size of the problem ahead of him, but rather on the size of the God he served! *He would think of his potential in terms of what God could do through him rather than what others thought God could not do through him!*

In those unrushed times with God he would have worked through his issues of insecurity. His soul was filled with the power of God. He was preparing for his calling. We know this because he emerged from this season of his life with *unusual courage.* He served from a soul that was *fueled* and *ready* for the next chapter of his calling.

What are the ways that you particularly connect with God and are filled with strength? Rearrange your life so that you can have times of refreshing in God's presence!

QUESTIONS FOR REFLECTION AND DISCUSSION:

1. Are you consistently setting aside time for God to speak to you and breathe fresh life into you through his Word? If not, think of the best time and place for you to make this happen.

2. Do you presently have encouraging, spiritually focused friendships in your life? Are you getting the consistent fellowship, worship and teaching that you need?

3. Do you feel like you are 'stuck' in your devotional life? What changes can you make to your present spiritual habits to bring a freshness to your quiet times?

CHAPTER TEN:
INCREASING YOUR PHYSICAL CAPACITY

Beloved, I pray that all may go well with you and that you may be in good health, as it goes well with your soul. (3 John 1:2)

I am more of a man than I used to be. And that is not necessarily a good thing! When we are younger it seems that we are invincible and that it does not really matter what food we eat and fitness choices we make. However, like every other area in life, our choices are leading us down a path towards a predictable destination. The predictable destination I have arrived at is that my chest is sinking down to my waist!

The older we get, the more intentional we need to get about lifestyle and health decisions if we are going to have a body that allows us to enjoy the best life has to offer. The *lack of care* for our bodies has a cumulative effect. Likewise, *caring for* our bodies has a cumulative effect.

I have many motivations at this stage in life. Firstly, now that I am in my 40's I am amazed at how much work it takes to drop a few pounds. If I do not take action now I will simply sink deeper and deeper into the couch and suffer the ill consequences of inactivity. Secondly, I want to keep up to my boys. I want them to have a dad that is able to run with them, coach them in their sports and go on adventures with them that are physically demanding. Thirdly, I am in the process of strengthening my knee after my second major surgery because of sports injuries (ACL reconstruction). Out of necessity I need to fortify my knee or I will end up with one toothpick leg. As painstaking as the process of rehabilitation is, I am finding that I can turn this to my advantage as it brings a focus and consistency to my work-out routine. Finally, I want to be as healthy as possible for as long as possible so I do not short-circuit what God wants to accomplish through my life. I have seen people do this and it is tragic!

God is concerned about the physical aspect of our lives. Paul, in 1 Tim. 4:7-8, while emphasizing that pursuing godliness is a higher value, still recognized the value of physical training. I want to 'max out' on my God-given potential and that requires having a body that can has vigour and stamina. As a believer you should aim to be physically healthy *so that you will have more in the tank to serve the Lord for as long as possible and as robustly as possible.*

Steven Covey in "*The Seven Habits of Highly Effective People*" gives an effective illustration of having the ability to sustain your call and reach your potential[16]. Although he applies it to the area of personal growth and development, it equally applies to maintaining and increasing your physical capacity. He uses Aesop's fable of the goose and the golden egg to illustrate that sustainability is everything.

> *This fable is the story of a poor farmer who one day*
> *discovers in the nest of his pet goose a glittering golden egg.*
> *At first, he thinks it must be some kind of trick. But as he*
> *starts to throw the egg aside, he has second thoughts and*
> *takes it in to be appraised instead.*
>
> *The egg is pure gold! The farmer can't believe his good*
> *fortune. He becomes even more incredulous the following day*
> *when the experience is repeated. Day after day, he awakens*

---

16   Steven Covey, *The Seven Habits of Highly Effective People*, Simon and Shuster: New York, NY, 2004, p. 52.

*to rush to the nest and find another golden egg. He becomes
fabulously wealthy; it all seems too good to be true.*

*But with his increasing wealth comes greed and impatience.
Unable to wait day after day for the golden eggs, the farmer
decides he will kill the goose and get them all at once. But
when he opens the goose, he finds it empty. There are no
golden eggs — and now there is no way to get any more.
The farmer has destroyed the goose that produced them.*

This story illustrates a natural law called the "P/PC Balance".
In this analogy "P" equals what you *produce* (i.e. — the "golden
eggs" that are your ability to be physically mobile, to enjoy recreation, and to work) and "PC" equals your *production capability*
(i.e. the "goose" that is your ability to continue to produce). *Your
production capacity is a gift from God and is something that needs to be
guarded carefully!* Most of the goals you have in life require that
you not squander it! When we eat processed foods, live a sedentary
lifestyle, carry extra weight and abuse substances that are harmful
to our bodies *we are decreasing our capacity.* When we take shortcuts
like relying on pharmaceuticals for ailments that could be treated
through exercise and diet we are *decreasing our capacity.*

Conversely, *we are increasing our capacity* when we eat healthy
food and consistently get active. It motivates me to think that an
investment I make into one part of my replenishment strategy will
have benefits in other areas. When I am physically energized it has
spin-off benefits in my earning capacity, my creative ability, my
family time, my sense of well-being, and even my ability to hold a
train of thought when I pray.

Think of the benefits that you will enjoy when you increase
your physical capacity. You will see a corresponding increase in
your overall well-being and ability to enjoy life. We need to have
a more holistic approach to wellness — because that is how we
were made! When you are well in one area of your life, the benefits
overflow into other areas of your life.

I also want to challenge you to think about how you can also get exponential returns when you combine different aspects of your replenishment strategy. For example, you can take a walk with your spouse, go for a prayer walk or go for a bike ride with friends. If you can find combinations that you truly enjoy you will have made great strides towards maintaining your motivation to be as healthy as possible for as long as possible.

In the warmer months our family prefers outdoor activities and chores to keep us active and mobile, whether that be gardening, hiking, or yard work. Unfortunately, the winter months are long in our part of the country and it is easy to slip into a sedentary lifestyle for a good portion of the year if one is not careful.

One of the best decisions I have made in my adult life was to begin a winter exercise regimen with my boys — now aged 17, 15 and 12. I have made several attempts at regularly working out in the past, but none of these efforts have netted lasting results. At best I have been a 'weekend warrior' that plays a bit of pick-up soccer, hockey, or football. At worst I have wished that watching a game on TV could somehow vicariously help me get back in shape!

Factors that have contributed to this new fitness regimen 'sticking' are:

A Fixed Time. We work out at a regular time each day (5 p.m.). In fact, as I am writing this chapter one of my sons just walked by and said "It is time to work out in a few minutes"! My 17 year old is filling up his water bottle. That's my cue that it is time for me to take a break from writing and whip this body into shape! The great thing about having a regular time to work out is that it helps you to get into a rhythm. There are days when we are out of town or we simply take a day off, but this one simple factor is helping us be consistent. You are setting yourself up for a profitable routine if you can eliminate any opportunity to talk yourself out of getting active on a given day. Once you get into a rhythm, you begin to plan other activities around your exercise time rather than never getting to your exercise.

Work-out partners. My boys and I have one another as work-out partners. When you have someone else helping you towards your fitness goals, the odds of maintaining the program increase dramatically. I don't know about you, but when it is time to exercise I can think of the most clever excuses to skip a work-out. Chances are that one out of the four of us will be motivated enough on any given day to say "It's time to work out!"

Dedicated space. We have dedicated a space in our basement for fitness. The climate we live in is inhospitable for getting exercise out-of-doors for several months of the year. We find it is easier to walk down the stairs than to pack up and drive to a gym — not to mention that it makes more economic sense (I would rather buy a used piece of fitness equipment and pocket the rest of the money rather than buy a gym membership!). This also helps remove the excuse we would have if we needed to shuffle items around a multi-purpose room. The space is only partially finished — but it is functional. We have dreams of making it a cooler "man cave" space, but for now we have to be content that the room will not make the cover of "*Muscle and Fitness*" magazine!

Equipment. No matter what you are doing, good tools help you avoid frustration and aid progress. This has not cost us a lot of money. Almost every piece of gear we have is used but in working condition. We bought a 'free weight' starter kit then added a few buy and sell items such as a treadmill, a recumbent cycle, a weight bench, a balance board, a skipping rope and exercise bands. For under $500 we have enough equipment for our whole family of five to stay in shape.

Music. For most people, music is a great boost to motivation. Do not underestimate this! When I went downstairs to work out with the boys today they had a song blaring with the lyrics: "*Whip it into shape. Shape it up. Get straight. Go forward. Move ahead…*". It is funny but it is motivating! Their music is a bit heavy for my taste but it definitely gets the adrenaline pumping. And we play it loud because we have no neighbours near enough to hear it!

Sometimes as we are dragging ourselves to the exercise room we hear whoever got there first hitting play on their iPod. It lights a fire under us to make it all happen again! Some people find synergy in their replenishment strategy by listening to podcasts while they work-out. Your exercise time will go by more quickly when your senses are engaged rather than just staring at a wall!

A Work-Out Plan. I am not a fitness expert, but I know enough to say with confidence that a good work-out plan is one *that you will actually do*! In my younger years I could always be motivated to exercise if I was playing a competitive sport. These days, the plan that works for me is one that includes a lot of variety and has elements of cardiovascular and weight training. For quite some time the only tool in my toolbox was jogging — and frankly that was simply too boring to hold my attention. So find out what types of exercise you will *actually* do consistently. Then have a plan in mind. A simple plan is preferable because, again, you want to make the process of exercising as automatic as possible. In the colder months we plan to use our fitness room and I play hockey, but in the warmer months we prefer outdoor activities (such as hiking and chores) to keep us active and mobile. Find what works for you and don't get discouraged when you get thrown off your plan!

To be honest, I get frustrated with the rate of change in my body after so many hours of hard work. Even when you are on the right path you do not often see the results you would like to see *when* you want to see them. That is when I need to remind myself that I am on the right path and that if I stay on it long enough I will enjoy the results. I regularly remind myself that it will pay off and that I will be on the right side of fitness consequences (as long as I can lay off of the chocolate)!

An analogy from the world of driving has helped me in this regard. Remember taking driver's education training? One of the first things I was taught about highway driving is that you can get yourself into trouble if you set your eyes directly in front of the vehicle rather than several hundreds of meters down the road.

This is especially a concern when following the highway around a bend. If you look directly in front of you, they told me, you tend to make more jerky steering movements, whereas when your eyes are focused further down the road your hands will take you more naturally and progressively to that destination.

The same is true of living a healthy lifestyle and getting more active. If I look at the results after three work-out sessions or even three months of working out I can get disheartened, give up and crash. Instead, I need to talk to myself (yes, talking to yourself is a tool emotionally healthy people use!). I speak to myself about what the results will be *after a full year of training*. I tell myself how good I will feel if I lose just a little more weight in that time period. I look further down the road rather than right in front of me. I tell myself that I will look good on the beach. Well, I might not look good on the beach but at least I will look better than if I had just stayed on the couch and ate Doritos!

I keep a quote in my office that is one of the most profound pieces of wisdom ever written: *We usually overestimate what we can do in one year and underestimate what we can do in five or ten years* (Ted Engstrom). The principle was written to stir leaders to take the long view of organizational impact, but its truth holds in the area of fitness and any other area of our lives. We live in a culture that promises and values quick results, but the universe is not built that way! If your eye is set on goals for feeling better and losing weight several months down the road you will be fuelled to take action today.

In past generations people were more physically active out of necessity. Modern conveniences, technology and prosperity have resulted in a more sedentary population. As a result, we need to be increasingly deliberate about getting active. We also need more convincing that the returns far outweigh the costs! Regular physical activity will help you:

- Tone muscles

- Improve your self-image

- Improve your posture

- Increase your energy levels

- Increase your heart and lung capacity

- Prevent loss of bone density

- Relieve stress

- Burn calories

- Prevent and more readily recover from injuries

- Keep weight off

- Reduce physical pain

- Improve your cognition

- Feel and look younger

- Brighten your mood (exercise has been called the best anti-depressant available[17])

I hope that this chapter will be a trigger that God uses to help you get on track physically and affirm the positive steps you are already taking. As I completed this chapter we were visiting friends and had a rousing game of pick-up football with them and some kids from the neighbourhood. I can honestly say that it was one of the best times I have had in a long time — and it is all due to maintaining and increasing physical capacity. Go for it! You can do this. Oh, and one more thing: I am happy to report that my chest is making it's way back up to where it belongs!

---

17   http://www.time.com/time/health/article/0,8599,1998021,00. html

QUESTIONS FOR DISCUSSION AND REFLECTION

1. What are your greatest motivations for staying healthy?

2. What foods or lifestyle habits do you need to drop that are having adverse affects on your health and well-being?

3. Write down your goals for being replenished physically.

CHAPTER ELEVEN:
CREATING A LIFE-GIVING MARRIAGE

Two are better than one, because they have a good reward for their toil. For if they fall, one will lift up his fellow. But woe to him who is alone when he falls and has not another to lift him up! Again, if two lie together, they keep warm, but how can one keep warm alone? And though a man might prevail against one who is alone, two will withstand him—a threefold cord is not quickly broken. (Eccl. 4:9-12)

Your marriage has the potential to be one of the greatest *drains* or *blessings* in your life! This chapter is all about *taking responsibility for your part in creating a marriage that is life-giving for you and your spouse.* It is about positioning yourself to enjoy the blessing that God intended marriage to be. This is a critical aspect of your replenishment strategy.

It was J. Allan Peterson who originally wrote about the fact that most people get married believing a myth! They believe that marriage is a beautiful box full of all the things they have longed for: companionship, sexual fulfillment, intimacy, friendship, laughter and financial security. The truth is that marriage, at the start, is an empty box. You must put some things into it before you can take anything out of it!

When it comes to building the kind of marriage that fortifies and feeds us, the outcomes are not as random as popular culture may lead us to believe. Every day we are making choices that move us closer to, or further away from, the marriage we dream of. What we put into the union is generally what we receive back. Yet people often fail to see this obvious connection. For example, a married man may routinely watch pornography and flirt with women at his workplace, and then wonder why he feels detached from his wife and why he is considering decisions that will forever scar his wife and children. Or, a married woman ignores her husband's need for attention, touch and respect but cannot for the life of her understand why he seems to be drifting away from her and why she does not have the fairytale marriage she dreamed of as a young girl.

MAKING CHOICES FOR YOUR MARRIAGE

Every day you need to make choices *for* your marriage. It will be difficult to feel that you are making any progress in your replenishment strategy if you are not diligent in this area, especially because *the threats to marriage are so great today.* The course of your marriage can be determined by your response as a couple to common potential threats:

- A person with striking looks and questionable motives strokes the ego of one spouse

- One partner makes a decision that hurts the family finances

- As the years go by one spouse's body changes dramatically because they let it go or because they struggle with a medical condition

- One spouse tastes success and gets pats on the back in their work life and the other is in a season of frustration in their vocation

- One partner wants to remain in the community where they have roots and the other wants to live more adventurously

- One spouse has a vibrant faith in Christ and the other shows little interest in spiritual matters

Each time a new threat or challenge is faced, the trajectory of the marriage relationship is re-set. Each time a decision is made *for* the marriage, the love, appreciation and richness of the relationship deepens. When you are willing to nurture your marriage daily, even when that is a difficult choice, you move one step closer to the marriage God envisioned for you.

TAKING GOOD CARE OF EACH OTHER'S HEARTS

During the days of my courtship and later engagement to my beautiful wife, we were often apart from one another for long stretches of time. As you could imagine, this put our hearts under some strain, in part because we craved each other's company, and in part because we were not naïve to the fact that all committed relationships face very real hazards.

Because my future wife was and is an amazing musician, I feared that in my absence she may become mesmerized by some musician guy with long greasy hair. He wouldn't have my astonishing good looks, but he may win her heart with a wicked "D" chord. On the other hand she may have wondered if I would fall for a team member or one of the many young adults we met as we criss-crossed Canada on ministry teams.

What was our solution? Before the travelling began I covenanted to take good care of her heart. She covenanted to take good care of my heart. *Then we followed through with our promise.* If ever we had feelings of doubt or insecurity we could always fall back on the promise that *the other was acting in our absence as though we were there in person.* When we spoke on the phone or wrote letters we would continually affirm each other with this truth. We would end our communication by saying, "I am taking good care of your heart!" That ended up forming an impenetrable wall of defence around our relationship. And if ever we felt we were losing resolve, we leaned on the strength of godly friends around us for support.

We would do anything to take care of each other's hearts — even if it looked comical at times. I remember in those days that we had a secret signal that would alert team members that we wanted rescuing from a conversation with a member of the opposite gender. We would just touch our hair in a certain way and a team member would swoop in and smoothly make a way of exit!

Wisdom tells couples to decide ahead of time to care of one another's hearts rather than waiting to see how they feel at the time. There will be days when you will not feel like staying on this pathway. To change the metaphor, we are always making investments and seeing returns on the kinds of investments we make. In Biblical language, we reap what we sow. Every good thing that you enjoy in your marriage today is the result of what you and your spouse have previously sown.

Only by staying on the path of love and loyalty do you reap the rewards. Only then can you savour and treasure moments like having a twinkle in your eye when your spouse enters the room even after many years of marriage or squeezing your spouse's hand at your child's wedding (knowing that instead of bending to outside pressure on your marriage, you stayed the course and provided a solid foundation for your children to build upon).

I'm getting a bit choked up as I write this in our local coffee shop. I want your heart to be moved as much as mine is. If you are married, *devote yourself in this moment to take good care of your spouse's heart.* This requires proactivity — do not let your love grow stagnant. Tell your spouse today that you are taking good care of their heart — and follow through with that by:

- having boundaries in place to protect the relationship

- treating your spouse with respect and tenderness

- eliminating anything in your life that is a compromise — even a small one

- investing quality time into the relationship

- verbally affirming your spouse

- reserving time for sexual intimacy

- finding mutually enjoyable activities

- building a network of friends that will support your marriage

- making your spouse a priority over your kids

- making your spouse a priority over your career

- allowing God to shape and re-shape your character

Your spouse deserves this — and God requires this.

But what if you are in a hard season in your marriage? What if the embers of first love are losing their glow? Then it is all the more important that, in a *sustained* effort, you make the investments into the marriage that will yield the results you want. Kind words. Pursuing each other. Giving each other the gift of time. Hot dates. You get the picture.

Does that mean that we get the results that we want every time? Not always, but we usually get favourable results if we stick with it over the long haul. Most people make a small effort for a couple of days, but that does not constitute putting the marriage on a course of wellness. *Most spouses will find a relentless pursuit of their hearts utterly irresistible.* However, there are cases where a spouse closes themselves off from the best and repeated efforts of their partner because they have hardened their hearts and chosen a path of self-destruction. If you have (or had) a partner like that it is even more vital that you get intense about every aspect of the replenishment strategies in this book. And if you are in an abusive situation, part of your plan should be seeking out professional counselling.

POSITION YOURSELF FOR A SATISFYING MARRIAGE

What are the mindsets and practices that result in a fulfilling and lasting relationship rather than in chronic disappointment or heartache? Here are some of the points of wisdom that have produced a healthy relationship with my bride of 20 years:

Determine that you will not discuss the 'd' word. It brings a lot of security into your relationship when you both know that even if things get really difficult for a season, you will never threaten each other with divorce or even entertain the possibility. In my experience, couples that speak openly about divorce are already taking a step down that path. Good marriages start with a commitment to forsake all others and provide a secure and safe space for love to grow (Matt. 19:6).

Keep dating and pursuing one another. The best defence in a marriage is a good offence. If your spouse feels treasured, supported and sexually fulfilled you are putting your marriage on a winning course. My wife and I have come to treasure our weekly date on my day off. It gives us the opportunity to unwind together and to have uninterrupted time to reconnect. The added bonus for us is that when we go to couple's events we can always win the 'most recent date' award! Do not let busyness give you a second-rate marriage. *Even when you are in seasons where there are more demands on your time, be sure that you take moments to embrace, acknowledge and affirm your spouse.*

Set boundaries in your relationship that protect it from outside interference. This includes what you expose yourself to online (this is a growing problem for both men and women). It includes how you will relate to the opposite sex in the workplace and being careful to not become emotionally intertwined with a member of the opposite sex other than your spouse. It includes putting distance between yourself and morally questionable people who take advantage of others when they are vulnerable.

Support one another in parenting challenges. During the years when children are young, *both* parents need to contribute, otherwise the task of parenting will prove to be overwhelming for one spouse. Also, in later years when children are challenging mom's authority, dad needs to step in and remind the children of how to speak respectfully and appropriately to their mom, and vice versa. Back each other! other. Never let your children's wishes cause division between the two of you. Solidarity on the parental team comes first!

Celebrate each other's accomplishments and milestones. The marriage relationship is no place for jealousy and envy. A vocational or personal 'win' for one spouse is a 'win' for both spouses. *If you are your spouse's biggest fan and cheerleader, you are setting yourself up for a rich marriage.* Your spouse has a longing and a need in their lives for you to celebrate them! Take time to celebrate the little victories along the way.

Bring the burdens of life together before God in prayer. Life can be overwhelming at times. There is power when a husband and wife bow together and agree in prayer. Take time to release God's ability into areas of your marriage and life in which you are aware of your inability. We carry unnecessary stress into our marriage when we do not cast our cares on the One who cares for us. I do not think you need to be hyper-spiritual to do this! It can mean just sighing a few words of simple prayer to God when your heads hit the pillow.

Be sure that you are in agreement on decisions that are made. In my marriage relationship I am the one that is more inclined towards making rash decisions because I enjoy a lot of change and variety. I have found that if my wife has reservations about my latest and greatest idea that I should listen to her insights. If you are not in agreement about a decision that goes bad, you end up not only with the mess that has been created from that decision — you also have the stress of repairing broken trust with your spouse.

Minimize financial stress. Many studies have confirmed the reality that every married couple knows from experience — *one of the greatest strains on a marriage is financial pressure.* Living beyond your means, incurring consumer debt and lack of communication are some of the common culprits. Put your heads together and prayerfully examine your budget. And if there is no budget to examine, it's time to make one! Determine together how much to spend on each area, being realistic about what actually comes in and needs to go out. More on this in the next chapter!

GREAT MARRIAGES ARE BUILT IN ORDINARY MOMENTS

As I look back on what I have written in this chapter, I realize that I have taken a very serious approach to the subject of marriage. This is fitting because I want to give you a sense of urgency and call you to action. However, I would like to close this chapter with lighter stories that illustrate how *great* marriages are created in the *ordinary* moments of each day.

The first story happened a few years ago when we were visiting our close friends at harvest time. As some of you know, this can be a nail-biting time when farmers rush to get a year's worth of investment off the field and into the bin. It was fun for me as I rode along in the combine with my friend to hear the banter among the harvest crew and marvel at the satellite technology they used. The best part of the day, though, was when the women brought lunch out to the field. I do not remember what they served, but I remember being amused when I noticed that the husbands and the rest of the crew did not seem to even notice our lovely attendants! They went on and on about this field being ready and that field needing two more days (and other such talk that a non-farmer has a hard time following).

Looking back on it, we should have taken our wives in our arms, kissed them on the lips and told them what a delicious meal that was! It was an ordinary moment on a busy day just like any other, but we were either too concerned about what the hired men might think or we were not tuned in to the gifts that were in front of us!

The second story happened recently after a live event that I spoke at and my wife sang at. Afterwards, as people were visiting and making their way to the parking lot, I got chatting with a friendly older lady. She gave the usual remarks about how she had appreciated what we presented, then she said something I will not forget for a long time. She said, "I got a lot out of your talk, *but what I really liked was how you looked at your wife!*" I did not see that coming! The funny thing is that I do not remember being particularly 'starry-eyed in love' that day. However, that is the stuff that great marriages are built upon — small acts of love on very ordinary days!

ELDERLEY COUPLE DIES HOLDING HANDS

The family of a couple that was married for 72 years said that their life together was a real-life love story. Even the tragic car accident that ultimately ended their lives could not separate them, as they had only an hour's separation between them in their passing, yet their locked hands never let go.

"They believed in marriage," Dennis Yeager, the youngest son of Gordon Yeager, 94, and wife Norma, 90, told MailOnline (Oct. 20, 2011).

The couple was married on the day Norma graduated from high school at a small ceremony at a family member's home, the expense of which was paid by Gordon's first pay cheque. The couple had four children, but tragically their two middle sons passed away in car crashes.

Despite their closeness and enjoyment of life together, their son admitted that at times his parents were "total opposites". Gordon was a socialite and Norma was a perfectionist who was more comfortable pouring over their business accounting records.

The couple celebrated a rare 70th wedding anniversary, and Gordon would continually say, "I have to stick around. I can't go until she does because I have to stay here for her, and she would say the same thing."

Late one day on a trip to town, Gordon mistakenly pulled out in front of another vehicle and they were struck. In the intensive care unit, their son found them laying beside one another holding hands, though not responsive.

That afternoon at 3:38pm, Gordon passed away with his wife and family beside him. The anomaly began though for the family, when Gordon's heart monitor kept beeping! They asked a nurse what could possibly be happening, and she pointed out that the couple's hands were still locked together. Her heart was beating through him and it was picked up through his heart monitor, the nurse explained.

One hour later, at 4:48pm, Norma died too. When their daughter was asked what life would have been like for them if only one had survived, she said, "Neither one of them would've wanted to be without each other. I couldn't figure out how it was going to work. We were very blessed, honestly, that they went this way."

Their son concluded, " I don't believe there was a big secret to their marriage. Sometimes one or the other would get mad but they worked everything out. In the end, they chose each other and that was it. They were committed."

Such is the beauty and benefit of an unwavering commitment to invest into your marriage!

QUESTIONS FOR REFLECTION AND DISCUSSION:

1. Do you feel that your marriage is on a good path right now or is it in desperate need of attention?

2. Do you daily make a point of showing your spouse affection and appreciation of some kind? List some specific ways that you can show love to your spouse this week.

3. Set aside some time as a couple to discuss what drains and fills each of you in your marriage relationship and do brainstorming about solutions you can work on together.

CHAPTER TWELVE:
DE-STRESSING YOUR FINANCES

Therefore do not be anxious, saying, 'What shall we eat?' or 'What shall we drink?' or 'What shall we wear?' For the Gentiles seek after all these things, and your heavenly Father knows that you need them all. But seek first the kingdom of God and his righteousness, and all these things will be added to you. " Matthew 6:31-33

God wants us to be blessed, to be saved from financial anxiety, and to know the joy of having enough to share liberally with others. He wants us to see the connection between how we handle money and our relationship to Him. *He wants us to see money as an asset that increases our capacity to fulfil our God-given mission in life.*

We learn about what is wise either through applying *wisdom* or through the painful teacher we call *consequence*. Most of the lessons I have learned about money have been learned the hard way! As a result I am currently in a season where I am learning as much as I can about finances. Since most people in our culture are in bondage to debt and a consumer mentality, it is critical that you get off of that stressful path and get control of your finances. De-stressing this part of your life not only frees you *from* anxiety, it also frees you *towards* doing what you were designed to do.

STEPS TO FINANCIAL PEACE

A good place to go to start de-stressing your personal finances is Dave Ramsey's "*7 Baby Steps to Financial Peace*". Since we decided to implement these steps our financial position has improved substantially. We have also felt more empowered and less vulnerable. The following is a summary of the steps[18]:

Baby Step 1 — $1,000 To Start An Emergency Fund. An emergency fund is for those unexpected events in life that you can't plan for: the loss of a job, an unexpected pregnancy, a faulty car transmission, and the list goes on and on. It's not a matter of if these events will happen; it's a matter of when they will happen.

Baby Step 2 — Pay Off All Debt Using the Debt Snowball. List your debts, excluding the house, in order. The smallest balance should be your number one priority. Don't worry about interest rates unless two debts have similar balances. If that's the case, then list the higher interest rate debt first. Once you pay off the first debt, throw those payments into the next debt and watch the momentum grow.

Baby Step 3 — 3 to 6 Months of Expenses In Savings. Once you complete the first two baby steps, you will have built serious momentum. But don't start throwing all your "extra" money into investments quite yet. It's time to build your full emergency fund, which should be 3 to 6 months of your cost of living.

Baby Step 4 — Invest 15% of Household Income Into Retirement Funds. When you reach this step, you'll have no payments—except the house—and a fully funded emergency fund. Now it's time to get serious about building wealth.

Baby Step 5 — College Funding for Children. By this point, you should have already started Baby Step 4—investing 15% of your income—before saving for college. Whether you are saving for you or your child to go to college, you need to start now.

---

18   http://www.daveramsey.com/new/baby-steps

Baby Step 6 — Pay Off Home Early. Now it's time to begin chunking all of your extra money toward the mortgage. You are getting closer to realizing the dream of a lifetime with no house payments.

Baby Step 7 — Build Wealth and Give! It's time to build wealth and give like never before. Leave an inheritance for future generations, and bless others now with your excess. It's really the only way to live!

As we have implemented these steps we have learned a lot along the way. We found that the hardest step was Baby Step 1. However, we found that once we got started our motivation level and sense of hope increased — thus increasing momentum for the next step. We also found that there is wisdom in starting Registered Education Savings Plans for your children as young as possible so as to allow them time to grow (and in Canada to take full advantage of the Canada Education Savings Grant).

As for expenditures, the ones that can often spoil your budget are the smaller expenses that accumulate through the month. Also, the times when you feel rich are the times when you need to apply the greatest restraint and foresight. There will be ebb and flow in your financial life, so you need to be careful to plan for times when your cash flow is not flowing or you have unexpected expenses.

INCREASING YOUR FINANCIAL INTELLIGENCE

Here are some principles I have been learning that will help you increase your financial intelligence. Do not be fooled by the simplicity of financial ABC's. If you learn the fundamentals you will be able to breathe easier and make real progress:

Avoid all debt except for debt on items that are expected to appreciate in value. The Bible says that the borrower is servant to the lender (Proverbs 22:7). Get out from under the *oppression* of debt as soon as possible. Commit to only going into debt for appreciating items such as a home or property. There was a season in our lives when the credit card became unruly and had to be entombed in a solid chunk of ice frozen in the freezer, only to be thawed out for emergency purposes. If your credit cards get you in trouble, cut them up and throw them away (or at least freeze them)!

Minimize the amount of money spent on consumer items that depreciate in value. This includes almost everything available in the marketplace! Watch for *quality used* items that are selling at or below market value. Our family loves thrift stores or a good sale. There's nothing more fun than coming home with a real treasure purchased at a fraction of market value. Some of the best-dressed people we know are just excellent thrift-store shoppers!

Focus on adding to your money or multiplying your money. Consider what you may be able to sell, a service you may be able to provide, an investment you may be able to make or a business you can launch that allows you to go forward financially rather than backwards. This requires being observant, creative and aggressive. The people that gain financial margin in their lives are people that always have an eye to adding to or multiplying their money. Ideally, you will do this in a way that is consistent with your calling, passions and knowledge base.

Get on the right side of compound interest. When you take a long term approach to saving, you allow years of compound interest to work in your favour, thus improving your financial future. For example, we realized recently that if our boys start investing just $2000/year, for 8 years, starting at the age of 19, with a return of 10%, they would net $1,035,148 by the time they reached 65! However, if they wait until they're 27 to start, they would have to invest the same amount per year until the age of 65 to net $883,185[19]. That's a total investment of $16,000 in the first scenario, compared to $78,000 in the second. On the other hand, if

---

19   *Smart Couples Finish Rich,* by David Bach (Doubleday Canada, 2003), p. 95.

you accumulate consumer debt, the interest that you will be paying will erode your financial future.

Read all that you can and listen to all that you can to increase your financial intelligence. Learn from people around you that have made good financial decisions. Ask questions and get good coaching. If you see someone at a financial destination that you desire, do the things that they did to get to that point. Read a few books that fuel your motivation in the area of your personal finances. (I would highly recommend anything by David Ramsey and David Bach as a starting point).

Be careful about what kind of financial mind-sets you allow yourself to adopt from your friends, family and associates. The people around you are often the greatest source of unhelpful financial thinking. They often have self-defeating approaches to money that we need to be wary of, such as: a poverty mentality (i.e. — we will never get 'ahead'), a commitment to appearing 'wealthy' (even if they can't support the veneer without crippling debt) or simply a mentality of spending every dollar that comes in (rather than positioning themselves for the future).

Be wary of what is reported about the economy in the media, which tends to create a financial climate rather than report on the financial climate. I no longer allow doomsday prophecies from the media to affect my mindset or bring a feeling of hopelessness. There are always opportunities to grow your money, enjoy life, provide for your family and have abundance *in any financial climate.*

Think like an entrepreneur. Take ownership of your financial future by thinking of ways that you can work for yourself or ways that you can proactively add value in your place of work. Begin to think of yourself as a *free agent* that is empowered and capable. The world is full of opportunity for those who want to add an income stream, improve an existing service or start a new venture. In today's job climate it is good to have options for your future even in you are in a job that appears secure.

In this discussion about finances, I want to be careful to mention that it is common for people to achieve success financially at the expense of relationships with the people closest to them and their relationship with God. While pursuing financial goals, *be attentive to the kind of person you are becoming in that pursuit*. There are many examples in the Bible of people who handled wealth well and many who handled it poorly. There is a big difference between *having money serve you* and *having money be your master!* Money is a hard task-master and serving it will certainly deplete you.

I also want to emphasize that, as with any area of life, the benefits of getting yourself on the right path financially are often not immediately felt. This is why so many people give up prematurely. It is critical that you get on course and that you stay on course. When I get discouraged about our financial position I remind myself that I am on the right path and that if I stay on the path I will be more than pleased with the destination. This is a lost art that came more naturally to previous generations that took a long-term view of their family's financial well-being.

I remind myself regularly that our family is on a financial path will pay dividends in the future. Because we have made sacrifices in order to become homeowners rather than renting, and because we have invested "sweat equity" into our home, we have the reasonable expectation that we will build equity over the long run. Because we have adopted a measured and often frugal lifestyle we have been freed up to bring our cost of living down, buy things that we really need and still have margins to make memories by going on family adventures. Because we have worked hard, our children will have an inheritance. Since we have gone without some toys that our peers clamour towards, we are able to have an emergency fund that gives us peace of mind. Finally, in establishing a "multiplying bank account" with the goal of growing the fund through selling products and services, I am improving our family's financial prospects. The fund is very small, but I am confident that if I stay the course it will be substantial in 5-10 years.

Although the topic of finances didn't come up often in my growing-up years, I have since learned a lot of valuable lessons that I am passing on to my children. In a sense, they will stand on our shoulders financially. I do not say this because they will have a large inheritance — I say this because they will understand the principles behind financial progress. Each generation can enjoy increasing financial stability as they utilize wisdom from the previous generation.

This is why, from a very young age, we have followed the advice of a former pastor and taught our children to divide any money that comes in into 3 jars. The first is for giving to God as an act of worship towards the One "who gives you the power to get wealth" (Deut. 8:18). The second is for long-term savings (for things that will retain value and help them meet their goals, like musical instruments and education). The third is for short-term savings (this is their fun money). I strongly encourage you to take the same approach with your children and with other children in whose lives you have influence. This is not a 'cute' idea! As our oldest son approaches graduation from high school I can see that he is well on his way towards a less stressful financial life because of the principles he has implemented.

EMOTIONAL BARRIERS

But how does all of this square with real life? To be brutally honest, this area of life is no different from others in that *discouragement always has to be fought against*. My experience tells me that getting on a good financial path has as much to do with winning emotional and mental battles as much as it does with developing skills like budgeting.

Common emotional barriers to financial well-being include:

Allowing envy of other's financial peace to make you feel depressed. Why not allow their progress to be fuel for your own financial dreams? If they made progress then so can you!

Feeling that the climb out of debt is too daunting. In truth, the climb is arduous and many people lose the emotional battle and prematurely abdicate. You *can* do this!

An unbridled attraction to products that you cannot truly afford now. Credit gives you the *illusion* that you can afford products and puts you in the position of living beyond your means. This is a very seductive move by marketers.

Equating your sense of personal worth with your financial position. This leads you into competing with others for the accumulation of the latest products and toys. Yes, adults do face peer pressure. This mindset also makes your happiness *conditional* on factors that are out of your control and your perceived level of prosperity in relationship to others.

Jeopardizing your financial health by taking an expensive vacation that you feel that you deserve or need. While taking time for restoration of the soul is important, emotional and physical health has more to do with our daily and weekly routines than the "cure all" approach many people attach to costly vacations. If our routines are not helping us maintain our overall health then it is easy to become vacation junkies and saddle ourselves with more stress.

Reacting rashly to immediate financial crises, rather than pausing and making the decision that makes for long range financial health. Our first thoughts and strategies that arise when we are in crisis are not often our best thoughts. Your emotions may tell you that you have only one option when wisdom is telling you that you have a dozen options or even hundreds of options! For example, after a recent incident, our primary vehicle was deemed to a total insurance loss. Our first instinct was to panic and get into a newer vehicle, but when we collected our composure we found that the best option was to keep our vehicle. We didn't gain that coveted new vehicle smell, but we ended up with cash on hand for extra repairs and we retained a vehicle that we do not need to make monthly payments on.

Having your ego stroked by accepting offers of higher levels of credit or by borrowing to have nice 'toys'. Offers of credit give you a false sense of empowerment. We have recently been getting quotes on re-financing our mortgage and have been offered extra secured and unsecured credit to the tune of about $100,000 because of equity gained on our property. If I felt the need to be a 'big man' it would be hard to turn down this offer to increase my 'buying power'.

Getting stuck emotionally on your current financial position rather than where your wise financial decisions are taking you. Focus your thoughts on how excited you will be when you reach each financial mile-stone. Focus on what you will be capable of then and allow that to help you overcome any impatience you may feel now.

This last point emphasizes one of the most important life skills we can acquire to de-stress our lives financially. *If you struggle with the emotional side of financial health, learn to mentally rehearse the benefits of financial vigilance.* Imagine how you will feel in twenty years after having positioned yourself well financially. Remind yourself of how good it will feel to help your kids with their education and to have a more comfortable retirement. Learn to take comfort from the fact that you are on the right path and that it will pay off in the end. Free yourself from the short-term thinking that has enveloped the culture around you!

GOD PROVIDES IN A VARIETY OF WAYS

Some of you are probably reading this chapter and are in great need of encouragement that your God is the God who provides. You may have had some financial setbacks, growing pains in your business, or you may be in a vocational ministry role that tradition-ally is on a lower pay scale than many other professions. You know that Jesus said that a man's life does not consist in the abundance of what he possesses, but you have real financial needs in your life right now!

The disciples of Christ also wrestled with issues like these. For example, when they wondered aloud if all of their sacrifice would be worth it, Christ affirmed that the blessings that they would gain in serving the kingdom of God would be far greater — *to be precise 100 times greater* — than any financial sacrifice they had made (Mark 10:30). Jesus reserves the right at any time to trump our best laid financial plans so that our lives and our resources can be used for His greater purposes. He ensures that those who align themselves with his purposes will be provided for.

When I began in ministry I did not have the support of my family or the resources of a sending church behind me. *Yet I discovered that God was faithful in providing for all my needs as I pursued His will for my life.* There have been times when God has provided through more 'natural' means such as supplying a job, a contract or a speaking opportunity, while at times God has provided through more 'supernatural' means.

One of those occasions that the later happened was when I was still in high school and felt a desire to go on to post-secondary studies to prepare for my calling. At the end of a service (in the church through which I had come to faith in Christ) I went to the front to spend some time in prayer and ask God to provide for me to go to Bible college. On my way out of the church a curious lady asked me "What were you praying about?". I told her and then went on my way. In the evening I returned to the church for another service and met the same lady in the foyer. She was smiling. She handed me a crisp $50 and said "Here is your first $50 towards going to Bible college".

Since that time we have seen many other financial miracles, including provision of funds to go on missions trips and supply things that our children have needed. Probably the largest provision that we have seen, though, happened in a way that amazed us. I was on my way home from a leaders retreat and seven hours away from home in another province when I lost power in my vehicle. There I was, stranded on the side of the road in the middle of winter trying to stay warm under a sleeping bag. I called a tow truck.

I had to get a motel room for the night while I waited for the parts to get shipped in. The next morning it was only after I had paid the $500 repair bill that the service manager at the dealership told me, "Sorry, we've just discovered that the engine block is cracked. Unfortunately your vehicle can no longer be driven." Unfortunate indeed! I was forced to take a long bus ride home, but during that ride I had a sense that Jesus may have a good surprise for us amidst the disappointment of losing our one and only vehicle.

In the end we had three surprises. The first was that friends in our church gifted us a small older model 'run-around' car. The second was that other friends in the church lent us their SUV for our family to go ahead with a planned vacation. The third surprise happened when relatives of ours felt that God wanted them to help us with a primary vehicle purchase up to a specific dollar amount. We were reluctant to receive this kind of help but we could see the obvious provision of God in this offer and it allowed us to get a good imported used vehicle large enough to carry our whole family.

This kind of provision is by no means the norm for us, but we are blessed by God to have had our needs met and beyond, through whatever means He chooses. Now we are in a different season of life where we are seeing God provide for us in a variety of other ways. We are learning that God does not want us to think that He is limited to providing for us in the same way He has in the past. Trust that God will provide. Notice the means of provision that He is making available to you now.

As you can imagine, I experienced some trepidation as I transitioned recently from being an employee to being self-employed. I was greatly helped one day as God brought to mind the words of Jesus in Matthew 6:25-26:

Therefore I tell you, do not be anxious about your life, what
you will eat or what you will drink, nor about your body,
what you will put on. Is not life more than food, and the
body more than clothing? Look at the birds of the air: they
neither sow nor reap nor gather into barns, and yet your
heavenly Father feeds them. Are you not of more value than
they?

It occurred to me that the way that God provides for the birds
is to make available to them what they need so that they can gather
it. He also provides the energy and the means for them to be able
to gather what they need. God is the provider but there is partici-
pation involved on our part. We have to *gather*. This releases us from
the fear that there would be nothing to gather. God provides us
with everything we need. All that we need to do is be attentive to
how He is providing, then go out there and gather it! In my case,
this helped me to have faith that He will provide in one way or
another. As we have positioned ourselves to have multiple income
streams we are aware that our current plan may work out just fine,
or we will discover that He wants to provide through another
means. This has helped me to have a renewed confidence in the
goodness and generosity of God. It also has made my life with God
an adventure of discovering where He wants me to gather next!

INCREASE YOUR INCOME

While it is important to start with the basics of bringing spending
under control, living within our means and conquering debt (all of
these will bring you financial peace), at some point you will likely
need to think about how you may be able to increase your income.
Now, *the heart of financial stress is usually not how much money we bring*
in but rather what we are doing with the money we make. However,
you may also need to consider ways that you can increase your
income and/or add more diversity to your income so that you are

prepared for changes in the economy, your employment or your family situation.

Before I give some practical suggestions as to how you may do this, I would like to share with you a principle that will help you develop the entrepreneurial thinking we spoke about earlier. It is simply this — *think in terms of the possibilities that your education and experience open up for you rather than being limited by your education and experience.*

What knowledge and skills do you have that are transferable to another area that will be rewarding and consistent with your calling? What are you positioned to do that will both be fulfilling and add an additional source of income? You may want to do freelance work or start a side-business. You may be able to offer services as a consultant in your area of expertise. Perhaps you would enjoy developing courses or information products. You may be able to provide a service in your area with little or no start-up costs. You might identify a course that you can take that can give you more skills and prepare you to add another stream of income into your family revenues. As you develop an eye for the options available to you, you will be amazed at how many opportunities you notice!

Here are some further ideas that David Bach gives for increasing your income by 10 percent[20]:

- Adopt the mindset that you are in control of your financial future

- Move towards action mode and away from complaint mode

- Get clear on the value that you add and what your strengths are

---

20   David Bach, *Smart Couples Finish Rich*, Doubleday Canada, 2003, p. 212ff.

- If you are self-employed, give yourself a 10% raise

- If you are self-employed, identify your best customers and bring in others just like them

- If you are employed by someone else, prepare to ask for a 10% raise by getting feedback from management as to what value you add to the organization, presenting an action plan for how you will add more value and, finally, practicing for and making the ask

- Pursue a new career opportunity with a better company[21]

WHAT YOU DO WITH MONEY = YOUR LEGACY

You get to choose the end of the story. If your money is used for self-interest, then when you die people will gather around your casket for a few moments, eat a few stale sandwiches and go on with their lives! There will be no legacy of changed lives echoing into eternity. Alternatively, if your money is used to honour God, provide for your family and bless the suffering, your life will have brought a taste of the kingdom of heaven to earth and you will have laid up treasures in heaven for yourself!

I need to be honest at this point. For many years I struggled with the concept of generosity. My concern was more about survival than it was about creating a legacy! Over time, I began to discover the surprising joy that comes from supporting a missionary couple, a Bible College, a summer camp or a sponsored child!

I want to have a legacy like that of Mary, an older lady in the church I first attended as a teenager. When she found out that I

---

21   The best job search process available can be found at http://www.48days.com/wp-content/worksheets/job-search-process.pdf. The process is also helpful for self-employed people who want to focus their business on their ideal clients.

wanted to go to Bible College but I didn't have a lot of support to do so, she caught me in the church lobby and gave me a crisp $50 bill- the first step in my education! I often think of how that small investment in my life was multiplied many times over as I have had opportunity to travel the world, motivating people to fulfill their God-given destinies!

Now here is something that you will never hear from the advertisers that scramble so desperately to relieve you of your money — *your generosity levels determine how blessed and refreshed you are in this life!* The Bible says "*A generous person will prosper; whoever refreshes others will be refreshed*" (Prov. 11:25 NIV). In other words, part of your replenishment strategy needs to include generosity!

And God is able to bless you abundantly, so that in all things at all times, having all that you need, you will abound in every good work. (2 Cor. 9:8)

QUESTIONS FOR REFLECTION AND DISCUSSION:

1. If you could rate your level of financial peace on a scale of one to ten, what would it be?

2. Do you currently have a budget that is working for you? What areas of spending need to be tweaked to match your current income?

3. If necessary, what are some ways that you can increase your income over the next couple of years?

4. How does generosity fit into your replenishment strategy?

CHAPTER THIRTEEN:
RE-FOCUSING ON YOUR CALLING

Jesus said to them, "My food is to do the will of him who sent me and to accomplish his work." John 4:34

"Do you know what you want to be when you grow up?"

Inevitably when I ask another adult that question we have a good laugh together! The truth is that the majority of people are dissatisfied with their work lives. Forbes reports that a startling number feel stuck and are unhappy in their jobs[22]:

- In the U.S. and Canada only 19% of employees said they were satisfied with their jobs. Another 16% said they were "somewhat satisfied." *But the rest, nearly two-thirds of respondents, said they were not happy at work.*

- Globally, between 28% and 56% of employees want to leave their jobs.

---

22 http://www.forbes.com/sites/susanadams/2012/05/18/
new-survey-majority-of-employees-dissatisfied

FINDING YOUR VOCATIONAL SWEET SPOT

Clearly, many people are struggling to find their vocational 'sweet spot'. That explains why people are making job and career changes at record rates. Others, having given up hope of finding fulfilling work, have resigned themselves to their fate and have to grit their teeth to find the motivation to go to work each day. *They postpone their lives until the weekend or until retirement.*

Here are some questions that can bring to the surface how we really feel deep down about the career trajectory we are on:

Am I making a living or am I making a life?

Does my current job allow me the opportunity to use my God-given strengths and abilities?

Am I elated or depressed at the thought of being in the same job in 5-10 years?

Is my enjoyment of work providing a lift to other areas of my life or is my dissatisfaction at work bringing a dark cloud into my existence?

Am I able in my current circumstances to provide for my family at the level I need to / want to?

Does my heart sink or soar when I start my work week?

When someone asks me what I do for a living do I feel that the answer is authentic to who I am?

Do I feel a sense of healthy pride in telling people what I do for a living?

Does my current employment support or work against the other goals I have in life?

If I was to chart the direction of my career in terms of satisfaction and impact would I say it is trending upward or downward?

Your answers to these questions are important in determining how intense a focus this area needs to have in your replenishment strategy. *Life is too short and opportunities are too vast for you to not move towards work that you find invigorating.*

You will be empowered to move confidently into work that is fitting and rewarding when you understand some basic truths about the call of God on your life.

THE TRUTH ABOUT CALLING

God is sovereign over all that He has made and He is purposeful in all that He does. Unfortunately many well-meaning people downplay God's *concern for* and *calling upon* certain individuals, families, churches and ministries. *This is not an accurate reflection of God's heart or of His creative power!* We have to get clear on these basic truths:

God has certain assignments that are common to all of His children. For example, it is His will that we pray without ceasing, that we live joyfully and that we give thanks in everything (1 Thess. 5:16-18). It is His will that we do justly, love mercy and walk humbly with our God (Micah 6:8) and that we give attention to the needs of orphans and widows (James 1:27).

God has created each one of us with a unique contribution in mind that He would have us make in our short time on earth. Jeremiah was called to be a prophet. Joseph was designed by God to serve as a government official. Paul was a tent-making, church planting missionary. David was a warrior, a worshipper and a leader. Others were given "ability, intelligence, knowledge and all craftsmanship to devise artistic designs" with which to serve God (Ex. 31:1-5). *Every person* — from the boy with Downs syndrome, to the soccer mom, to the executive — *has been positioned by God to fulfill particular purposes that God has in mind for them!* "For we are God's handiwork, created in Christ Jesus to do good works, which God prepared in advance for us to do" (Eph. 2:10).

God has given us specific personality traits, aptitudes and desires that are clues to that unique mission. While it takes time, understanding and patience to fully comprehend our life mission, God does leave clues along the way! Where do your passions and aptitudes meet?

Where do your strengths lie? What clues lie in your uniquely created personality?

God is in control of the process — so we can rest in His plan. God can see the big picture while we see only one step ahead. God's timing is different than our timing, and His ways are higher than our ways. God is a good Father. You can relax and enjoy the journey rather than holding your breath until you feel that you have everything figured out!

God is able to take all of the events and experiences of my life, both good and bad, and weave them together so that I can have maximum influence for His glory. This point should give you great encouragement! God is so powerful that He can take even *the very events and words that were intended to hurt you or to thwart your life mission and use them as the means through which your life mission will be fulfilled!*

God has the ability, as you walk in fellowship with Him, to impact the lives of other people through you. We long to have lives of significance. In John 15, Jesus assured the disciples of this very thing when He said that *if they would abide in him they would bear much fruit to the glory of the Father.* It would take time. They would not always be aware of when it happened. They would have to entrust the outcomes to Him. But if they were in alignment with Him and living in dependence on Him, *fruit would happen.*

You need to focus on these *truths*, not the *facts*. If you focus on the facts such as, *I am not getting enough contracts right now* or *the economy is depressed in my region* you will lack the mental fortitude that you require. You will be vulnerable to opinions and events that are outside of your control. But if you focus on truths about God and his active involvement in your life, you will be more inclined to see obstacles as mere speed bumps instead of mountains! You will take on the attitude of an *overcomer* in your vocation. You will seek creative and innovative solutions. You will have the courage to take ownership of your work life and defy any odds that are against you.

For example, a good college friend of mine that was hungry to achieve more with his life's work experienced a major setback. He was in a car accident that left him with a brain injury that altered his moods and patterns of thought. He could have given up on his dreams of owning his own fitness studio and training mixed martial arts (MMA) fighters while influencing them towards Christ. But he did not give up. Everyday he filled his mind with the above truths. He surrounded himself with people who believed in him and had the expertise he needed to recapture his life. Truth sustained him as he endured the long path of rehabilitation. Today he is living his dream. When he speaks, people listen (not just because he knows MMA moves!).

Getting clear on the truths about the call of God on your life will help you to *avoid*:

Aimlessness. You will know what you have been designed for.

Insecurity. You can rest in the fact that what you are doing is significant in the eyes of God.

Wasted years. Every moment will contribute meaningfully to the whole of your destiny.

Frustration. A sense of fulfillment and empowerment comes when you are on God's unique path for your life.

Being controlled by the agenda of others. You will know more precisely where you are going and you will be able to identify diversions.

FINDING WORK THAT YOU LOVE

As a result of the truths above, I believe that *we have God's permission and directive to pursue work that we love.* Have you found work that is consistent with how you are designed? You will thrive more doing certain types of work and working in certain environments than in others. How many people do you know that can honestly say they thrive in their work environment? I am not saying that we will never have difficult days, but I do believe you will honour God the most and be the most happy when you move towards work that you are designed to do, rather than simply working for a pay check.

Here are *the six "A's" of finding work that you love*:

1. *Aim High*

We know that you get what you aim for in archery and lawn darts, but we often do not see this reality at work in the accomplishment of our life goals. When someone fulfills a life goal we sometimes mistakenly think:

- I *wasn't born with the same advantages so I can't achieve that goal*

- I *am not lucky like they are*

- I *am not naturally gifted like they are*

- *If I aimed at the same target I would surely miss*

The truth is that if you were to give the same care, attention, preparation and focus towards hitting that target you would accomplish a similar end. You can hit the target for your vocational goals if you consistently are aiming your efforts in the right direction.

We are not all provided with the same level of opportunity in life, but we must not use this as an excuse. There are likely many people in the world who are more poorly positioned than you — *and yet they still hit that desired target!* With determination, consistent effort over a period of time and with God's help we *can* be enriched in every part of our lives.

How many high quality, talented, personable people are getting beat up in work cultures in which they are not valued? How many people could be the boss but are unaware of it, or too afraid to achieve a higher level in life? The parable of the talents in Matthew 25 teaches us to take all that the Master has invested in us and proactively multiply it. *It pleases Him when we take our gifts as far and as high as they will take us!*

If I have learned anything in this season of life it is this: do not sit there waiting for the phone to ring with news of a great opportunity for you. Instead, take the steps, make the calls, submit the proposals and build the network so that you please the Master with *the initiative you take* and *the faith you exercise.* Take responsibility for what you do with your calling. Refuse to make the pursuit of your calling contingent on what another person does or does not do. If your ideal work situation does not yet exist, perhaps you can create it!

Much of what I am enjoying at this stage of my vocational journey (including the book that is in your hands) is the result of switching to a proactive approach to my calling. Author Jack Canfield captures the principles of initiative and proactivity when he urges his readers to *do five specific things every day to move you towards your goals.* Do what you can do and trust God with the outcomes.

My friend influenced my thinking with regard to aiming high by how he approached his education. He did not ask "What is the easiest route I can take?" Instead, he asked "How far and how high can God take me in my educational journey?" In the end he studied at a world class university and through a divine appointment built a personal connection with a member of that country's royal family. Instead of setting your sites low, *what might happen if you opened yourself up to God taking you to a greater level of influence?*

You may find it amusing (and hopefully inspiring) to know that when I re-read this story I got on the phone and set in motion my application to a *better* university for my PhD studies! I am excited at the prospects of this program and how it can be leveraged in a greater way for the kingdom of God. I am learning to go as far and as high as I can with what God has invested in me — *and I hope you will do the same.*

2. Alignment

We will not love our work every moment of every day even in the best of scenarios. However, people that are happy with their work will say that *their strengths, giftings, desires and values substantially align with their work*. Greater alignment means that you are doing fewer tasks that deplete you and more that energize you. It means that your goals and desires fit well within the larger context of the organization. When you experience alignment you are in a zone where you are more than happy to put in extra hours on a project. You are not concerned with punching a time clock. *You have internal motivation that fuels you and helps you overcome obstacles.*

A famous line from the movie "*Chariots of Fire*" illustrates this. When Eric Liddell is attempting to explain to his sister that he believes he has been designed by God for both missionary work and running in the Olympics he says: "I believe that God made me for a purpose. But He also made me fast, and when I run, *I feel His pleasure.*" This is the zone you want to be in! When you find vocational alignment you sense God's pleasure and a sense of 'rightness'.

Here is a simple test that will help you measure the degree of alignment you have. Imagine that you are meeting a new acquaintance and you are telling them what you do for a living. If your heart sinks at the thought of this then you probably have an alignment issue and you need to re-think your vocational path! If your heart begins to soar then you are on the path to having substantial alignment.

But finding work you love is not just about working within your field of interest. Within any field or industry you can find yourself in a workplace that either matches or runs contrary to your values, so it is also important to find the closest match with the culture of the organisation. Is the culture progressive or conservative? Is integrity valued or are indiscretions tolerated? Is complaining standard or are leaders honoured? *You will find that you are consistently drained if your work world does not match your most treasured values.* What is most important to you in your work environment? I have come to hold clear the following values that I use as an evaluation grid in determining the work I pursue and the partnerships I form:

- *freedom to creatively discover how to accomplish the mission*

- *camaraderie, support and friendship with colleagues*

- *making a difference locally and globally*

- *continually improving outcomes and relationships in the organization*

- *flexible approaches to work scheduling*

- *visionary leadership*

- *working with enthusiastic people that have a propensity to "buy-in"*

With values such as this it would be tragic for me to work in an environment that was critical, controlling, petty or — on the other end of the spectrum — passive, indifferent or fearful of change. *The level of satisfaction we derive from work is in direct relationship to the degree of alignment of our work with our values.* Working with people that share your values can be a little slice of heaven, while working with people that are in opposition to your values can be a little slice of…. well, I think you get the picture!

In addition to alignment with our values we also need alignment with our life mission. It is helpful to make time to look at the indicators that point you to a deeper understanding of God's unique purpose for your life, including your passions, spiritual gifts, competencies and personality (for a detailed description of this process get my free ebook "*Have More Purpose by Friday*" at *robparkman.com*).

Do not fall into the trap of just working for money. You will never find delight and purpose in your work life if you are only enduring your day to day existence. When I realized I was making mistakes in this regard I threw myself into finding work that I love. One of the best resources I found in that journey was tapping into Dan Miller's vocational wisdom, inspiration and resources at *48days.com*.

3. *Affirmative Colleagues*

In a "Peanuts" cartoon, Lucy asks Charlie Brown, "Why are we here on Earth?" Charlie replied, "To make other people happy." Lucy replied, "Then why are *they* here?!"

At the beginning of my career I had an older and wiser gentleman say "Be kind to people, because you never know who you may end up working with!" That statement is packed with vocational wisdom that will serve you well, for *the quality of relationship you have with people with whom you work is one of the leading factors in your level of job satisfaction or frustration.*

My theory is that when we are earlier on in our careers, we are in more of an experimentation phase. We are actively discovering what kind of work environments we enjoy, what types of people we prefer to work with and what types of endeavours bring us delight. When we are further along in our career we have a whole portfolio of life experience that informs which scenarios we should avoid and which we should pursue.

Judicious people consider how they can improve existing relationships, or alternatively, how they can get into a different work environment that has a more positive relational culture. When you work with people that have strong relational skills, characters of integrity and kindness, and a commitment to help you be at your best, then you are able to go to higher levels of productivity and fulfillment.

4. *Adequate Income*

While I encourage you to dream big when it comes to your life mission, you do need to ensure that you are bringing in enough income to meet your commitments. If this is not the case then you will not be sustainable and you will not have peace. I am smiling to myself as I write this because I am currently about one year into a transition into entrepreneurship, having left a job that provided a comfortable salary and benefits. I am constantly re-thinking our financial model and finding ways to make the work that we love sustainable!

This point may seem like common sense to you but you would be amazed at how many people have a vision to change the world but have not found a financial model that sustains that vision. They end up spending precious years of their lives doing work that they do not love or doing work that they love on an inadequate salary. If you can take your vision and find a fitting financial model, then you are well on your way to a vocation that fuels you.

The cost of living is rising so rapidly that this requires sustained diligence and focus. In order to ensure having adequate income to sustain your dreams and callings you may need to invest in a piece of equipment or a course that will increase your earning capacity. You may need to bring your expenses down dramatically. You may need to change your job or take on extra work for a period of time. You may need to seek out partners that will help make the dream a reality. You will have to work hard and you will have to work smart. *You will have to find ways to attain and maintain financial viability.* Your dream is worth it!

Michael Hyatt asserts that the three components that must be present for you to experience job satisfaction are: (1) *you must have passion,* (2) *you must be competent,* and (3) *you must have a market.*[23] If you have all three of these components — passion, competence, and a market — you experience satisfaction. Few things in life are more rewarding. However, *you have to be wary of having only two* because:

---

23   http://michaelhyatt.com/049-the-3-components-of-job-satisfac-tion-podcast.html

Passion + Competence - Market = *A Hobby*

Passion + Market - Competence = *Failure*

Competence + Market - Passion = *Boredom*

5. *An Attitude of Worship*

Brother Lawrence, in the book *Practicing the Presence of God,* spoke about how he worshipped God as much in his kitchen duties as he did in the special times of prayer in his monastery. He had a God-ward orientation in his work. Col 3:17 says, "And whatever you do, in word or deed, do everything in the name of the Lord Jesus, giving thanks to God the Father through him."

Chances are, there will be times in your life when you are in a less-than-ideal work situation, or that even within the pursuit of your dreams, parts of it will involve things you don't love to do! This is where attitude is everything. Your work, when it is unto the Lord, can be and should be an act of worship! Bring God into whatever you are doing, with your heart and mind set on him as you work. Continually ask for his help strength and blessing through the day. Look for ways that you can be a blessing to others in your work-place, and look for ways that you can bring glory to God through your work.

6. An Ant's Work Ethic

In Proverbs 6:6-8 we read: "Go to the ant, O sluggard; consider her ways, and be wise. Without having any chief, officer, or ruler, she prepares her bread in summer and gathers her food in harvest." Later in Proverbs 30:24-25 it says, "Four things on earth are small, but they are exceedingly wise: the ants are...not strong, yet they provide their food in the summer."

You will find much more enjoyment in working whole-heartedly than when you are only working half-heartedly! Rejoice and be thankful for the gift of work, and that through your efforts you are helping to provide for yourself and your family. When you work, you eat! At the same time, your work ethic can be an example to others and it can increase your options for the future. You will find deep levels of satisfaction as you work in a diligent and concerted effort towards outcomes that you value.

TRANSITIONING WELL

If you need to make a vocational change or upgrade be sure that you transition well by:

Building your ramp. Once when I was realizing that my work context was not good for me, I went to a man of God for advice. He said to me with prophetic insight, *"Build your ramp!"* There is a lifetime worth of wisdom in those words. Essentially he was telling me not to make a hasty move now that I realized a change needed to be made. He was telling me not to be reactionary, but to take a planned approach to the transition. As a result of his advice I made plans to move on, but not before I took months of careful preparations so that I had a 'soft landing'. I had tried the 'hard landing' approach in the past and found it to be highly overrated! Building your ramp looks different in each context, but it may include: communicating and planning with your spouse, exploring alternative options, gaining new skills or certifications and planning the best time to make your decision public.

> *"The plans of the diligent lead surely to abundance, but everyone who is hasty comes only to poverty." (Prov. 21:5)*

Considering your timing. No job lasts forever. Eventually you need to discern when it is time to transition out: "For everything there is a season, and a time for every matter under heaven" (Eccl. 3:1). Often people leave a job prematurely before they have gleaned everything they could have gleaned. On the other hand, it is possible to stay longer than you should in an unhealthy situation. This requires counsel. If and when you feel it is time to transition out of your current role, it is crucial that you surround yourself with people whose counsel you trust implicitly.

> *"For lack of guidance a nation falls, but victory is won through many advisers." (Prov. 11:14)*

Maintaining peace. It is normal to hit points of frustration in your work life, and there are times that you need to move on to something that is a better fit for you. However, far too often people take shots at the organization, or the people they were working with, as they are on their way out the door. In our thirst for vengeance we burn the bridge and close the door to relationships and opportunities with those people. This is 'shooting yourself in the foot'! Remember that you may need a reference from that company. You do not want to brand yourself as a malcontent. Additionally, some people end up wanting to return to the organization at a later date. Even if there were outstanding issues or concerns, be sure that you exit with grace and 'take the high road'. If there is any residual relational tension to deal with make sure you move towards that awkwardness. Having the difficult conversations will give you a greater sense of resolution and peace of mind. It will also prevent you from carrying the issue into your future.

> *If possible, so far as it depends on you, live peaceably with all. (Rom 12:18 emphasis mine)*

BUT WHAT ABOUT SETBACKS?

I would like to offer a few words of encouragement for those who have faced daunting setbacks in their vocational journey. For me, the story of Joseph is an inspiring story that demonstrates how God can even use dramatic difficulties to advance His calling on our lives. One of the first facts we learn about Joseph is that his brothers "hated him and could not speak peacefully to him" (Gen. 37:4). He is rejected by his brothers. Though they should have protected him, they sold him into a life of dreary servitude. Then, although he had proven himself to be a valuable and loyal slave, he is falsely accused of making sexual advancements on his boss's wife and thrown in jail for years. Finally, he has his hopes dashed again when someone who was positioned to help his cause totally forgot about him (Gen. 40:23).

As the story unfolds, Joseph begins to realize that he has been strategically placed by God to save the lives of his family and countless others from a terrifying famine. He comprehends that he was not a victim of the cruelty or neglect of people, rather he was an important player in the plan of God. *He was located by God for maximum impact.* He is positioned in the Egyptian government to save his family and untold thousands of lives. *Events that could have been interpreted as setbacks were actually advancing him towards his God-given calling.*

He finally discloses his insight to his brothers, saying, "It was not you who sent me here, but God" (Gen. 45:8) and "*you meant evil against me, but God meant it for good, to bring it about that many people should be kept alive, as they are today*" (Gen. 50:20). Amazingly, this insight into the workings of the providence of God *freed Joseph from bitterness towards his brothers and released him to show them kindness* (Gen. 50:21).

When Joseph has a poetic blessing spoken over him by his dying father, we receive insight into the secrets of his victories. Remember that, *even in the face of thorny problems and deep pain:*

Fruitfulness and kingdom influence are possible. "Joseph is a fruitful bough" (Gen. 49:22). Problems could not stop God's impact through his life- they only enhanced it.

Ongoing replenishment is available. He was "a fruitful bough by a spring" (Gen. 49:22). He had positioned himself for continual refreshing.

Prevailing empowerment is accessible. "The archers bitterly attacked him, shot at him, and harassed him severely, yet his bow remained unmoved; his arms were made agile by the hands of the Mighty

One of Jacob... by the God of your father who will help you, by the Almighty who will bless you" (Gen. 49:23-25).

In the end, the blessings that were brought into his life began to have a healing effect in his life, so much so that it completely overshadowed the affliction he had seen ("God has made me forget all my hardship" Gen. 41:51). In spite of all that he had been through, and because of all that he had been through, he was now positioned for great honor, impact and abundance.

The question that has to be asked is this — what would have happened if Joseph had become disillusioned and given up on the process? The redemptive potential of his life would never have been reached.

Be careful that you do not make the mistake of thinking that *this* chapter of your life is the *last* chapter of your life. Do not lose heart! God's redemptive power is greater than you realize!

YOUR GREATEST IMPACT MAY ARISE FROM YOUR GREATEST PAIN

Wes Stafford in *Too Small To Ignore* says that *the very area in your life that has brought you the most pain is often the area in which you have the opportunity for the greatest life impact.* You become the most passionate about helping others out of the suffering that you yourself have walked through.

He tells the heart-rending story of horrific abuse that occurred at the boarding school he attended. It was out of that agony and anguish that he emerged with a fiery determination to protect children at all costs. He became a champion of orphaned, mistreated and overlooked children all over the world as the president of Compassion International. At the time of writing, *over 1.5 million children are being set free from poverty in Jesus' name* through child-sponsorship! What the enemy had meant for evil against Wes Stafford, God had meant for good and for the saving of many lives.

I have seen these same dynamics at work in my own vocational calling. *I have seen how seasons of the most severe testing have been transformed for my benefit, for the benefit of others and for the glory of God.* For example, the startling experiences that I have seen in the people-helping business now fuel a burning passion to encourage, support and coach leaders who are on the front-lines trying to make a difference in the world. Now I am overcome with gratefulness that the Lord has opened doors for me to speak at leadership events at home and abroad. With God's help I pray that I will leave a trail behind me of leaders who have received new strength, strategies and renewal that will sustain them for the long haul.

It may be that some of your greatest passions and contributions in life emerge from the fires of adversity! Think in terms of the possibilities that your experience brings rather than the limitations. What difficulties have you walked through in the past that may hold a key to your future impact? Look at your life from a fresh perspective. All of your life experiences can be redeemed!

A BLESSING OR A CURSE — YOU DECIDE

One of the most draining things that you can subject yourself to is labelling a decision or a season in your life or career as a 'failure'. Sure, it may have been a stupid thing that you did. I know I have made more than my fair share of mistakes! You are not going to get it right 100% of the time. *More devastating than a bad decision though, is allowing yourself to live under a cloud because of that decision.* Regret saps us! Regret is living under the lie that our mistakes or misfortunes are too big for God to handle.

I am saying this to myself as much as I am saying this to you — *remember that God can do amazing things with the raw materials of your life.* The only thing that prevents that from happening is when you think that He can't! Then you are too busy being upset to know that He is up to something good. When you open yourself up to the possibility that He can bring out of the ashes something that is beautiful, *you will gain crazy amounts of energy and confidence!*

The story of the white horse told by Dan Miller has helped my wife and I to process events positively and with faith. I pray that it will help you gain new perspective for your journey.

"Like most everyone today, I have been hearing a lot of examples of hardships this week. No jobs, no retirement funds, worthless stock, cancelled vacations, new violence and political unrest, and general uncertainty. Rather than trying to create something profound I'd like to share this old story.

Once there was an old man who lived in a tiny village. Although poor, he was envied by all, because he owned a beautiful white horse. People offered fabulous prices for the horse, but the old man always refused. "This horse is a friend, not a possession," he would respond.

One morning the horse was not in the stable. All the villagers said, "You old fool. We told you someone would steal that beautiful horse. You could at least have gotten the money. Now the horse is gone, and you've been cursed with misfortune."

The old man responded, "Perhaps. All I know is that my horse is gone; the rest I do not know. Whether it be a curse or a blessing, I can't say."

After fifteen days the horse returned. He hadn't been stolen; he had run away into the forest. Not only had he returned, he had brought a dozen wild horses back with him. Once again the village people gathered around the old man and said, "You were right — what we thought was a curse was a blessing. Please forgive us." The old man responded, "Perhaps. Once again you've gone too far. How do you know if this is a blessing or a curse? Unless you can see the whole story, how can you judge?" But the people could only see the obvious. The old man now had twelve additional horses that could be broken and sold for a great deal of money.

The old man had a son, an only son. He began to work with the wild horses. Unfortunately, after just a few days, he fell from a horse and broke both his legs. Once again the villagers gathered around the old man and said, "You were right. The wild horses were not a blessing; they were a curse. Your only son has broken his legs and now in your old age you have no one to help you. You are poorer than ever." But the old man said, "Perhaps. Don't go so far. Say only that my son broke his legs. We have only a fragment of the whole story."

It so happened that a few weeks later the country went to war with a neighboring country. All the young men of the village were required to join the army. Only the son of the old man was excluded, because he had two broken legs. Once again the people gathered around, crying because there was little chance their sons would return. "You were right, old man. Your son's accident was a blessing. Our sons are gone forever."

The old man spoke again. "You people are always quick to jump to conclusions. Only God knows the final story."

And so it is with our lives. What we see as a blessing or a curse may simply be part of God preparing us for what lies ahead. Be careful in seeing "disaster" in any change. Just recognize it as change — which opens the door for good as well as bad — for gain as well as possible loss.

I've spent 25 years seeing people go through unexpected and unwelcome change — and have enjoyed seeing most move on to more opportunity, freedom, fulfillment and income.

What experience have you had — where initially what seemed a curse turned out to be the beginning of a blessing?"[24]

I am excited about the redemptive potential in your story. You've got this!

24 http://www.48days.com/2013/05/07/
blessing-or-curse-you-get-to-decide

QUESTIONS FOR DISCUSSION AND REFLECTION

1. Most people will have encountered something in their career path that has either felt like a set-back, a delay or a disappointment. Consider Rom. 8:28: *"And we know that in all things God works for the good of those who love him, who have been called according to his purpose."* List the blessings that have come into your life or how God may be increasing your sphere of influence through these experiences.

2. To what degree would you say that your current work provides alignment with your God-given purpose?

3. What steps can you take this week to further close the gap between your ideal work and what you are doing now (i.e. — getting career coaching, having a crucial conversation with a supervisor, sending out your resume, etc.)?

4. What is your replenishment strategy for your work life?

CONCLUSION:
BECOMING RESILIENT

He raises the poor from the dust and lifts the needy from the ash heap, to make them sit with princes, with the princes of his people. (Ps. 113)

As kids we would make our way out to a local park each summer. The park was known locally as "The Springs" because of a naturally occurring flow of water that would come out of the hillside and pool before draining into the river. We were drawn in and mesmerized by this phenomenon! I was struck with boyhood wonder. *There in my own backyard was a place that I could go and drink cool clean water whenever I wanted to!* I have never tasted such refreshing water since.

I want you to know that God has provided you with a means of constant replenishment similar to what we found as kids at "The Springs". *By His Spirit He makes available to us a never ending supply of living water* (John 7:38-39). You are well resourced. He has provided for you all that you need to be continually refreshed! You are provided with all that you need to fulfill your life mission. All that you must do is *access the resources that God has already made available,* whether you are receiving what you need directly from Him or by some means that He provides.

When you do so, you become resilient and unstoppable. You always have ways to get regenerated, rehydrated and repaired so that you can move forward confidently. The apostle Paul speaks of this. He and his team faced a lot of draining effects as they zigzagged across the then-known world proclaiming the gospel, including challenges to their authority, shipwrecks, jail time, and financial scarcity. Yet, in spite of all of this, *they had found God's means of continual renewal*:

> So we do not lose heart. Though our outer self is wasting away, our inner self is being renewed day by day. (2 Cor. 4:16)

TRUST THE PROCESS

Back in "Part One" I mentioned that at one point a whole host of draining effects converged on my life at once. It was an emotionally intense season that made me fear for my own health. I was bewildered. I felt alone. I felt betrayed. But thank God, *that was not the end of the story!* I want you to know that, without exaggeration, *I worked my replenishment strategy every moment of every day.* For the longest time I did not feel the results, *but I trusted the process.*

After what seemed like an eternity I could see the light at the end of the tunnel. My dark night of the soul was coming to an end. The cumulative effects of seeking replenishment began to be felt and seen. I started to hope again. I started to be free of baggage from the past. I started to dream again. I could feel confidence and joy returning. I had clung to the Lord (by my fingernails at times) and *He had proven himself faithful.* I say this to let you know that I have been living the replenishment strategy in this book. I can say with full confidence that *if you work the plan, the plan will work for you.*

One of the inspirations for my own comeback was the story of Drew Brees in his book *Coming Back Stronger: Unleashing the Power of Adversity.* Drew Brees was an NFL quarterback with a bright future ahead of him when he sustained a serious shoulder injury.

His team at the time, the San Diego Chargers, were hesitant to give him guaranteed money in his contract and weighted the bulk of the contract towards performance incentives. They had lost confidence in their starting quarterback because of the injury. Other teams entered talks with Brees, but doctors all over the league warned their teams that Brees may have already seen his best days on the field.

These were difficult days for Brees as he was dealing with recovery from surgery, contract uncertainties and a sense of rejection from his team. The New Orleans Saints was the only team who would take a chance on Brees. As a city they had just experienced the trauma of Hurricane Katrina. Not only was the city devastated, but likewise was the team as it was forced out of its stadium and ended the previous season with a dismal record. The football club was an underdog. The city was an underdog. Drew Brees was an underdog.

When all of the odds were against him, Brees focused on the things he could control. He could control his focus on rehabilitation, he could choose to keep his faith in God alive, he could retain an optimistic outlook and he could hone his skills daily to position himself for the best possible outcome. Brees, the Saints and the city of New Orleans then set out to show the world just how resilient they could be! With Brees at the helm, the record of the team began to improve and the city began to regain its swagger.

Finally, all of the effort to push through hardship was rewarded as the Saints were victorious in Super Bowl XLIV! Brees was named as the Super Bowl Most Valuable Player *and* as the Sports Illustrated Man of the Year for both his play on the field and his extensive charitable work that supported the restoration of the city.

Brees says that the key is "trusting the process". That means that *he would do everything in his power during the preparation phase* to ensure that he could compete at the highest level possible. Then, when the pressure came, all of the physical, mental and spiritual preparation would take over and bring him the results he was looking for!

When it comes to getting refuelled, trust the process. It will take time. You will have bad days. You will have doubters. However, if you string together enough small, prudent restorative decisions together, eventually you will have your own comeback story!

A PORTRAIT OF RESILIENCY

I have a friend who is a poster child for this kind of jaw-dropping resiliency. He and his wife had returned home from a high adrenaline posting on the mission field so that she could have a much-needed rest. He was working in the construction industry for modest wages when a well known "Christian" leader and a "Christian" real estate developer approached him with an investment deal "he could not refuse". It was a no-brainer: they were fellow believers offering *amazing* returns.

Sadly, it was all a scam.

My friend did not realize this until it was too late. They quickly made off with his money and that of seven other unsuspecting families (to the tune of one million dollars). My friend lost $225,000 plus $25,000 in interest charges for a grand total of a quarter of a million dollars.

You can imagine the fallout in his life. His wife no longer trusted him. She separated their finances and stopped going to church with him. She did not know if she was going to stay with him. He had made a mistake and had dug a large, gaping financial hole. His once vibrant faith in Christ took a beating because he had been defrauded by people claiming to be genuine Christians. He fell into a pit of despondency for six months. In the past he had enjoyed intimacy with God and had regularly heard the voice of God speaking to him and directing him. Now he heard nothing. He did not want to live.

It was then that he showed up one Sunday at a church I was serving at. He heard the voice of God say to him, "This is not the end! You can recover from this!" "How?" he responded incredulously, "The bank owns my house except for my down payment. My wife does not trust me and she may not stay."

Two weeks later he was back at , church where there happened to be a presentation about the difference Compassion sponsorship makes for a child living in poverty. My friend heard the voice of God again, saying, "*This* is your opportunity to recover!" This made my friend mad, but he angrily agreed to do what God said and committed to sponsor a child from a Muslim family in Burkina Faso. He definitely did not know where the money was going to come from.

One week later he heard that familiar voice saying, "*Is that all that you can do?!*" This time he softened to God's voice. Although he was bewildered about how this made financial sense, he said to the Lord, "I'm glad you are still talking to me". He marched over to the Compassion table and committed to sponsor six orphaned boys and six orphaned girls! He knew that he did not have that kind of money, but he also knew the voice of God.

Now the story gets really crazy! The very next week, the site supervisor for the company he worked with moved on, leaving my friend to take over his role. My friend was shocked and amazed to get his first monthly cheque for $12,000. That was *three times* what he had been making previously! Within four and a half years he had recovered financially and had wiped all debts off his books, including his mortgage! In the meantime he ventured into his own construction business and added another four sponsored children.

I talked to my friend yesterday to get an update on his life and to ask his permission to include his story in this book. I was so happy to hear that God had not only helped him to recover financially, but now his marriage has also been restored! He and his wife are attending church together again and they are even dreaming about doing more missions work in their retirement years. In addition, my friend deliberately hires young men who are fatherless and broken, so that they can get mentored and trained, become free of addictions, provide for themselves and become a contributor in the workplace. Oh, I almost forgot to mention, he also has a vision to increase the number of Compassion children they sponsor to one hundred and twenty orphans![25]

I remember working with my friend and doing some sailing with him *during* his recovery. Before he knew what all of the outcomes were going to be, *he worked his replenishment strategy.* He decided the financial setback would not define him. He had made a mistake but he would recover. He worked hard. He made good decisions with his money. He worked to regain the trust of his wife. He chose to have a positive outlook on each day. He worshipped God *out loud* wherever he went! When he went to church he spread joy to others and chose to be enthusiastic in his praise.

He became resilient because he realized that nothing had really changed!

God was still good.

God still had a plan for him to be a person of kingdom impact.

God could refuel him each and every day and send him on his way rejoicing.

Now, go and do likewise!

---

25   If you are inspired by my friend's story to sponsor a child go to my Compassion Ambassador site: www.compassion.ca/ambassador/ robparkman

REPLENISHMENT RESOURCE ONE —
MY REPLENISHMENT STRATEGY

Instructions:

1. *Identify the areas that are in greatest need of replenishment in your life:*

2. *Indicate the steps that you will take to get refuelled in each area.*

Renewing Your Mind

Forgiving Your Debtors

Choosing Your Friends = Choosing Your Future

Giving Yourself Permission to Rest

Nourishing Your Spiritual Life

Increasing Your Physical Capacity

Creating a Life-giving Marriage

De-stressing Your Finances

Refocusing On Your Calling

REPLENISHMENT RESOURCE TWO —
REPLENISHMENT VERSES

But you , O LORD, are a shield about me, my
glory, and the lifter of my head. (Ps. 3:3)

I believe that I shall look upon the goodness of the LORD
in the land of the living! Wait for the LORD; be strong, and
let your heart take courage; wait for the LORD! (Ps. 27:14)

O LORD my God, I cried to you for help, and you
have healed me. O LORD, you have brought up my
soul from Sheol; you restored me to life from among
those who go down to the pit. (Ps. 30:2-3)

You have turned for me my mourning into dancing, you have
loosed my sackcloth and clothed me with gladness. (Ps. 30:11)

Oh, how abundant is your goodness, which you have
stored up for those who fear you. (Ps. 31:19)

The LORD preserves the faithful but abundantly
repays the one who acts in pride. (Ps. 31:23)

I will bless the LORD at all times; his praise shall
continually be in my mouth. (Ps. 34:1)

Those who look to him are radiant. (Ps. 34:5)

When the righteous cry for help, the LORD hears and
delivers them out of all their troubles. (Ps. 34:17)

Your steadfast love and your
faithfulness will ever preserve me! (Ps. 40:11)

God is our refuge and strength, a very
present help in trouble. (Ps. 46:1)

We have thought on your steadfast love, O God. (Ps. 48:9)

But I am like a green olive tree in the house of God. I trust
in the steadfast love of God forever and ever. (Ps. 52:8)

Cast your burden on the LORD, and he
will sustain you. (Ps. 55:22)

Blessed be the Lord, who daily bears us up. (Ps. 68:19)

You who seek God, let your hearts revive. For the
LORD hears the needy and does not despise his
own people who are prisoners. (Ps. 69:32–33)

Gladden the soul of your servant, for to You,
O Lord, do I lift up my soul. (Ps. 86:4)

Satisfy us in the morning with your steadfast love, that
we may rejoice and be glad all our days. (Ps. 90:14)

Because he holds fast to me in love I will deliver him; I
will protect him, because he knows my name. When he
calls to me, I will answer him; I will be with him in trouble;
I will rescue him and honor him. With long life I will
satisfy him and show him my salvation." (Ps. 91:14–16)

[The LORD] satisfies you with good so that your youth is renewed like the eagle's. (Ps. 103:5)

For he satisfies the longing soul, and the hungry soul he fills with good things. (Ps. 107:9)

He raises the needy out of affliction. (Ps. 107:41)

Those who plan peace have joy. (Prov. 12:20)

A tranquil heart gives life to the flesh, but envy makes the bones rot. (Prov. 14:30)

Stop regarding man in whose nostrils is no breath, for of what account is he? (Is. 2:22)

Tell the righteous that it shall be well with them, for they shall eat the fruit of their deeds. (Is. 3:10)

You will keep in perfect peace him whose mind is stayed on you, because he trusts in you. (Is. 26:3)

The meek shall obtain fresh joy in the LORD. (Is. 29:19)

For thus says the One who is high and lifted up, who inhabits eternity, whose name is Holy: "I dwell in the high and holy place, and also with him who is of a contrite and lowly spirit, to revive the spirit of the lowly, and to revive the heart of the contrite." (Is. 57:15)

My soul continually remembers it and is bowed down within me. But this I call to mind, and therefore I have hope. The steadfast love of the LORD never ceases; his mercies never come to an end; they are new every morning; great is your faithfulness. (Lam. 3:20-23)

To set the mind on the flesh is death, but to set the
mind on the Spirit is life and peace. (Rom. 8:6)

Forgetting what lies behind and strain-
ing forward to what lies ahead. (Phil. 3:13)

Set your minds on things that are above, not
on things that are on earth. (Col. 3:1)

May the Lord direct your hearts to the love of God
and to the steadfastness of Christ. (2 Thess. 3:5)

Set your hope fully on the grace that will be brought to
you at the revelation of Jesus Christ. (1 Peter 1:13)

REPLENISHMENT RESOURCE THREE —
RECOMMENDED READING

Action Trumps Everything, Charles Kiefer, Leonard Schlesinger and Paul Brown (Duxbury: Black Ink Press, 2010).

Boundaries, Henry Cloud and John Townsend (Grand Rapids: Zondervan, 1992).

Clout, Jennifer Catron (Tennessee: Tomas Nelson, 2014).

Get Out of That Pit, Beth Moore (Nashville: Integrity, 2007).

Happiness is a Choice, Frank Minirth and Paul Meier (Grand Rapids: Baker, 1978).

Healing the Masculine Soul, Gordon Dalbey (Dallas: Word, 1988).

Increasing Your Personal Capacity, Eddie Windsor (Tulsa: Insight Publishing Group, 2004).

It's Not My Fault, Henry Cloud and John Townsend (Nashville: Integrity, 2007).

Jesus Calling, Sarah Young (Nashville: Thomas Nelson, 2004).

Leaders Who Last, David Kraft (Wheaton: Crossway, 2010).

Leading On Empty, Wayne Cordiero (Bloomington: Bethany House, 2009).

Learning to Tell Myself the Truth, William Backus (Minneapolis: Bethany House, 1994).

Making Life Rich Without Any Money, Phil Callaway (Eugene: Harvest House, 1998).

Margin, Richard Swanson (Colorado Springs: NavPress, 1992).

Necessary Endings, Henry Cloud (New York: Harper Collins, 2010).

No More Mondays, Dan Miller (Colorado Springs: Waterbrook, 2008).

Pastors At Risk, H.B. London and Niel Wiseman (Wheaton: Victor, 1993).

Pastors In Transition, Dean Hoge and Jacqueline Wegner (Grand Rapids: Eerdmans, 2005).

Replenish, Lance Witt (Grand Rapids: Baker, 2011).

Reposition Yourself, T.D. Jakes (New York: Atria, 2007).

Reposition Yourself — Reflections, T.D. Jakes (New York: Atria, 2007).

Safe People, Henry Cloud and John Townsend (Grand Rapids: Zondervan, 1995).

Say "Yes" To Your Potential, Ross and Carlson (Waco: Word, 1983).

Smart Couples Finish Rich, David Bach (Doubleday Canada, 2003).

The Emotionally Destructive Relationship, Leslie Vernick (Eugene: Harvest House, 2007).

The Healing Path, Dan Allender (Colorado Springs: Waterbrook, 1999).

The Principle of the Path, Andy Stanley (Nashville: Thomas Nelson, 2008).

The Rest of God, Mark Buchanan (Nashville: Thomas Nelson, 2006).

The Slight Edge, Jeff Olson (Lake Dallas: Success Books, 2005).

The Total Money Makeover, Dave Ramsey (Nashville: Thomas Nelson, 2007).

We Are Driven, Robert Hemfelt, Frank Minirth and Paul Meier (Nashville: Thomas Nelson, 1991.

Wounded By God's People, Anne Graham Lotz (Grand Rapids: Zondervan, 2013).

Your Ministry's Next Chapter, Gary Fenton (Grand Rapids: Baker, 1999).

**SHARE THE REFUEL EXPERIENCE
BY GOING TO
WWW.THEREFUELEXPERIENCE.COM!**

Get everything you need to fill the tanks of your **small group, leadership team or entire church.**

Visit **ROBPARKMAN.COM** for more information, resources and live events that will help you **REFUEL!**

CPSIA information can be obtained at www.ICGtesting.com
Printed in the USA
LVOW10s1950281115

464356LV00001B/7/P